The Clinician's Guide to Anxiety Disorders
in **Kids** and **Teens**

STRATEGIES • ASSESSMENTS • TOOLS • EXERCISES • HANDOUTS

PAUL FOXMAN, PH.D., Author of *The Worried Child*

Copyright © 2017 by Paul Foxman, PhD

Published by
PESI Publishing & Media
PESI, Inc
3839 White Ave
Eau Claire, WI 54703

Cover: Amy Rubenzer
Editing: Marietta Whittelsey
Layout: Bookmasters & Amy Rubenzer

Printed in the United States of America

ISBN: 9781683730330

All rights reserved.

This therapist guidebook is dedicated to my mother, who served as a school psychologist for over 30 years in some of the most challenging school districts in New York City. My mother believed that every child is worthy of respect, support and an opportunity to achieve his or her highest potential. Her unwavering commitment to improving the lives of children has been a source of inspiration for this book.

About the Author

Dr. Paul Foxman is Founder and Director of the Center for Anxiety Disorders, a private outpatient practice and therapist-training center in Burlington, Vermont. He has over 40 years of professional experience in a variety of settings, including schools, community mental health centers, graduate psychology programs and private practice.

Dr. Foxman is also the author of *Dancing With Fear* (2007) and *The Worried Child* (2004), as well as other publications on the topic of anxiety including a co-authored casebook, *Conquering Panic and Anxiety Disorders* (2003). Dr. Foxman travels internationally to speak on the topic of anxiety, and he has appeared as an expert on radio and television. Dr. Foxman is known for his knowledge and clarity of thought, sense of humor, and engaging speaking style.

Dr. Foxman's training includes Yale University (B.A. in Psychology), Peabody College of Vanderbilt University (Ph.D. in Clinical Psychology), pre-doctoral internships at the Department of Psychiatry at Mt. Zion Hospital in San Francisco and the Kennedy Child Study Center in Nashville, and training seminars at the San Francisco Psychoanalytic Institute.

In 1985 Dr. Foxman co-founded the Lake Champlain Waldorf School in Shelburne, Vermont, now flourishing from kindergarten through high school.

Table of Contents

Chapter 1 — Initial Assessment and Relationship Building 1
    Before the First Appointment
    Establishing Credibility
    The First Appointment
    Initial Interview with Young Children
    Anxiety Screening Tools
    Standardized Anxiety Measures

Chapter 2 — Creating a Treatment Framework and Language 25
    "Three Ingredients" Framework
    Explaining Anxiety to Children

Chapter 3 — Foundation Skills for Managing Stress and Anxiety 35
    Behavioral Health Recommendations
    Three-Step Approach to Stress Management
    Relaxation and the Magic Word Technique
    Breathing Games and Practices
    Mindfulness Skills for Children and Adolescents
    Meditation for Preschool Children
    Yoga for Young People
    Flow Activities

Chapter 4 — Interventions for the Anxiety Disorders 59
    The *DSM-5®* Anxiety Disorders
    Co-occurring Disorders (Depression, Attention Deficit-Hyperactivity Disorder, Behavior Problems)
    Separation Anxiety
    Generalized Anxiety Disorder
    Panic Disorder and Agoraphobia
    Obsessive-Compulsive Disorders including Trichotillomania and Excoriation
    Social Anxiety
    Selective Mutism
    Specific Phobias
    Trauma- and Stressor-Related Disorders

Chapter 5 — Medication and Nature's Remedies 99
    When to Refer for a Medication Evaluation
    Pros and Cons of Medication
    Herbal Treatments
    Homeopathic Remedies

Chapter 6 — Involving Parents in Treatment 107
    Therapeutic Alliance with Parents
    Managing Risks in Divorce Cases

Acknowledgements

I thank PESI for inviting me to prepare this guidebook for therapists and counselors who work with anxious children and adolescents. I also appreciate PESI's confidence in sending me to every state in the U.S. to teach mental health professionals, educators, speech and language pathologists, occupational therapists and other professionals how to recognize anxiety in children and help them heal. It has been a successful and gratifying collaboration that I hope will continue with this book.

Saul Neidorf, M.D., a child psychiatrist, was an influential mentor who served as a role model for how we can work authentically and creatively with children. His recent passing was a profound personal loss. I know he would be proud of this book and I wish he were alive to see me carry on his legacy.

I am grateful to the Kennedy Child Study Center in Nashville, Tennessee, one of the training sites that activated my interest in working with children. If you want to grow as a therapist, try being observed by colleagues and teachers through a one-way mirror and critiqued afterwards.

Introduction

As a graduate student in clinical psychology over 40 years ago, I interned at the Kennedy Child Study Center in Nashville, Tennessee, where I began to specialize in child psychotherapy. Among many lessons and insights, I learned that the most important ingredient in successful work with children is the therapeutic relationship. Children know intuitively which adults "get them," and who they can trust with their symptoms and stories. This guidebook is designed, in part, to help therapists tune into the experience of anxious children and to "connect" with them as an essential step in effective therapy.

An emotional or behavioral symptom in a child is a *story*. Anxiety, for example, is a form of communication about the effects of stress. Embedded in the story are the feelings, thoughts and perceptions about what a child has experienced in the family, school and/or community. In this therapist guide to addressing anxiety in children and adolescents, you will find approaches that can help children reveal their stories as well as how you can respond in helpful and healing ways. Your success in reducing anxiety and related symptoms in children depends in large measure on how you understand and work with a child's story.

My training and experience with child therapy spans four decades and includes an array of approaches. Beginning with my foundation in psychoanalytic psychotherapy, I have explored cognitive-behavioral therapy, solution-focused therapy, psychodrama and gestalt therapy, meditation and mindfulness practices with children, bodywork approaches including yoga and martial arts, expressive arts therapy, family systems, bilateral brain stimulation techniques, and other interventions. This therapist guidebook includes many of these approaches and you are encouraged to experiment with them. You can use the following principle in applying new approaches to working with children (as well as adults): "If an approach might be helpful and is unlikely to be harmful, feel free to experiment with it."

I have organized the process of child anxiety therapy into treatment phases, each of which is represented by a chapter in this book. ***Generally speaking, there is a sequence of phases involved in effective anxiety treatment with children. These include the following:***

1. Initial assessment and relationship building

2. Create a treatment framework and language

3. Introduce skills for stress management and anxiety control

4. Apply appropriate strategies, techniques and interventions based on the type of anxiety involved

5. Medication considerations (including "nature's remedies")

6. Involve parents in child therapy, including special circumstances where parents complicate treatment due to parent anxiety, divorce and other issues

Chapter 1

Initial Assessment and Relationship Building

Establishing Credibility Before the First Appointment

Children and adolescents are referred for therapy by a variety of sources, including:

- Schools
- Pediatricians and family physicians
- Insurance company provider lists
- Employee assistance programs
- Other therapists
- Web sites
- Other clients
- Word of mouth

How do these referral sources view you? What is your reputation as a therapist? Are you a new therapist in the community or are you established as a known and respected professional? Are you viewed as a child-friendly therapist? Are you known for your specific style or approach to therapy (play therapist, CBT therapist, trauma specialist, parent educator) or for the population with whom you work (children, families) or for the problems you address (anxiety, ADHD, spectrum disorders, behavior problems)?

These questions are important, because one of the variables in the effectiveness of therapy is your credibility. Clients, especially parents of child clients, are influenced by your reputation and credibility. If you are seen as an expert child therapist you are more likely to have positive outcomes due to the "expectation effect." While you should not exaggerate your skills or outcome effectiveness, you will receive more referrals and do more effective work if you are viewed as a competent clinician. How can you improve your reputation and credibility?

There are several ways to establish credibility as a child therapist. These include:

- Having a web site with an appealing professional profile
- Professional profile on Internet referral sources (e.g. *Psychology Today*, Health Service Providers in Psychology, state professional organizations, Anxiety Disorders Association of America)

- Giving free talks on relevant subjects such as anxiety in children, managing children's social media use, stress management skills for children, dealing with separation anxiety or school refusal, etc.
- Writing brief articles for local newspapers on subjects related to children and adolescents
- Podcasts on subjects related to children and adolescents

Of course, there is no substitute for good work. No amount of advertising or marketing will improve your skills or help you "connect" with your clients. Nevertheless, your effectiveness will be influenced by your clients' expectations and those expectations come through the door before you initiate therapy. Below are some recommendations for establishing credibility, along with some specific examples.

Establishing Credibility with Children and their Parents

Your relationship with child clients begins with the first telephone contact with parents. In many cases, parents have questions about how you work, the techniques you use, your experience level, how long therapy will last and your success rate with similar cases. These are valid questions and parents who are informed or sophisticated about therapy are more likely to ask them.

To address these questions, and to establish credibility with parents, I suggest you prepare a narrative that describes how you work. Some therapists present their professional narrative in web site listings as well as in the consent-to-treatment and disclosure forms that parents sign at the outset of therapy. Here are two sample professional profiles from child and adolescent therapists at the Center for Anxiety Disorders in Burlington, Vermont:

Sample Child Therapist Profiles

Leslie London, M.A., Leslie has a unique gift for engaging children in therapy and guiding parents in developing sensitive communication skills. Her office is a virtual playroom where children use play and creative expression as their natural way to communicate their feelings and needs. Dedicated and caring, Leslie uses the relationship she develops with each child and the therapeutic powers of play to help children grow and change. She responds to the particular needs of the child and family, recognizing that in therapy parents remain the most important influence in their child's life. Leslie helps parents to better understand their child's emotional difficulties and how to mobilize the child's healthy desire to mature.

Leslie is a psychology intern working toward licensure under the supervision of Paul Foxman, Ph.D. She earned her Master's degree in clinical psychology at Saint Michael's College and draws on over 40 years of experience as a child development specialist and early childhood educator.

Stephanie Haney, LICSW, Stephanie is a licensed clinical social worker who specializes in working with children. She is also a licensed school social worker and school adjustment counselor in Massachusetts. In addition, she holds a graduate certificate in autism spectrum disorders from Antioch University in Keene, New Hampshire.

Stephanie has worked with children as a psychotherapist, social skills group facilitator, camp program director and educational consultant in public schools. She has served as

> a case manager for students with Individual Education Programs (IEPs) and conducted clinical observations and assessments of individual students and whole classrooms. An important part of her work is to provide emotional and psycho-educational support to teachers and parents. Stephanie uses a strengths-based approach and draws from cognitive-behavioral, narrative, play and art therapy techniques to promote the psychological, emotional and social well-being of her clients. She provides individual, family and group therapy to children, families and adults. Her areas of expertise include anxiety, depression, social-cognitive challenges, autism spectrum disorders, self-esteem, bereavement, stress and family and interpersonal relationship issues.

The First Appointment and Initial Interview

Research on therapy outcome has found that the effectiveness of psychotherapy is attributable to the following variables (Wampold, 2008; Lambert, 1992):

- 30% therapist-client relationship
- 40% client motivation
- 15% therapist expectations
- 15% therapist techniques and theoretical orientation

This research tells us that your techniques and theoretical orientation are not the most important variable in therapy effectiveness. Instead, the quality of the relationship between therapist and client—the therapeutic alliance—is a more influential source of change and healing. Therefore, you should invest in developing rapport, trust and credibility with your clients, and this begins at the first appointment (if not before in term of your reputation and credibility as discussed above). When working with children and adolescents, you actually have two clients: the child/adolescent and the parents. In divorce cases, you may even have three clients, especially in high-conflict families where there are two co-parents who may be at war with each other.

The first step in therapy is usually an initial interview. With young children, the first appointment can be a parent interview without the child to obtain a developmental history, details about symptoms, and the concerns of the parent(s). Many therapists prefer to interview the parent and child together at the outset of treatment. In either case, a semi-structured interview approach is advised.

There are two goals for the initial interview:

- To assess the child client and family in preparation for treatment planning
- To establish rapport and credibility with the child and parents so that they will be inclined to engage in therapy with you

These two goals need to be approached sensitively. It is more important to "connect" with the child and parent(s) in the first few appointments than to complete a prescribed intake form. The relationship takes precedence over the background information to be obtained early in treatment. It is reasonable and appropriate to spend several appointments obtaining the data required for diagnosis and treatment planning.

With adolescents, you might begin the initial interview with the parents but then spend time with the adolescent alone. It is important to balance an alliance with the parents and confidentiality assurances to the adolescent. This may require some discussion with and education of the parents, so they will understand the therapeutic value of confidentiality while trusting they will be informed about any high-risk behaviors or other safety issues.

Semi-Structured Initial Interview

When meeting initially with child clients and their parent(s), a semi-structured interview is the most productive format.

One purpose of the first appointment is to **obtain sufficient information for an accurate diagnosis and appropriate treatment plan**. However, the first appointment is also the beginning of the therapeutic relationship. Remember that the relationship is the highest priority. Therefore, I advise the therapists on my staff to take several sessions if necessary to obtain the database for treatment while investing in rapport, trust and credibility with young clients and their parents.

It is advisable to ask parents to prepare their child for an initial appointment. You might suggest they address their child with some variation of the statement, "Erica, I've noticed how worried and upset you've been lately and I've made an appointment for us with a man/woman who works with children who feel just like you do. He/she is a counselor." Advise against terms such as "doctor," "psychiatrist," and "psychologist," as these labels can sometimes stimulate a fear reaction in a sensitive child.

Include the parent (or both parents if available) in the initial interview, especially with young children. It is not advisable to include siblings in the office as they may distract, tease, or otherwise inhibit the child's communication. Family therapy may be part of the treatment plan, to begin at a later point in time.

A semi-structured initial interview is the most widely used screening method for children with anxiety. This approach is flexible, natural, and comprehensive. Begin with an open-ended question, such as, "I'd like to know what is going on that led to your being here today." Then direct a question to the parent, such as, "Since you called to make this appointment, let's start with you. You must have some concerns that prompted you to call me."

Typically, the parent will talk about what is currently going on, and you can probe the response for details about the presenting problems. Note behaviors and symptoms, such as school refusal, separation anxiety, difficulty going to sleep without a parent in the room, unwillingness to perform in class, social avoidance, poor eye contact, and other difficulties. Follow-up with direct questions as needed to obtain a full symptom picture. Some areas to explore include:

- Is Erica having any trouble at school?
- If so, when and in what way?
- Is there a particularly difficult time of day, such as mornings or nighttime?
- How does Erica get along with other children?
- Is she shy or intimidated by other children?
- Does she have any close friends?
- Are there any other concerns we have not discussed?

During this stage of the interview, turn to the child every few minutes and ask for input about the parent's comments. Seek information that reveals the child's feelings, cognitions, and physiology. Try asking questions, such as:

- Do you agree with what your Mom just said?
- How do you feel inside when...?
- What do you think your Mom is most worried about?
- What are your thoughts when you...?

For "I don't know" responses, you can help by giving sample responses and begin to show empathy by asking questions, such as:

- Do you feel nervous, like an upset stomach or like something bad is going to happen?
- Do you sometimes think, 'What if certain bad things happen...like 'What if I get kidnapped?' or 'What if something happens to my parents?' or 'What if other kids make fun of me?

Your goal for the initial interview is to determine the following:

- The child's normal affect
- The child's affect in response to specific cues or stresses
- The specifics of the child's anxiety responses
- The child's thinking process
- The nature of any physical symptoms

After obtaining a thorough symptom picture, a developmental history is the next step. Some clinicians provide a developmental history form to the parents before the initial interview and review it at this point in the meeting. If you are taking the history in the session, it might be helpful to go through each stage (pregnancy, birth, infancy, toddler, preschool) and ask for examples of behaviors or developmental milestones. Developmental questions include:

- As an infant, was Erica highly sensitive to lights, noise, or medicine?
- Was she a worrier or easily upset?
- Did she object to being left alone at night?
- As a toddler, did she follow you around from room to room?
- Have there been any unusual illnesses or medical issues?

Toward the end of the initial interview, leave time for a summary of the anxiety condition and your general recommendations for treatment (for example: education, relaxation practice, CBT, exposure).

> A dry-erase board or easel can be helpful in conveying your ideas about what is going on and what might be helpful. A positive and encouraging attitude is essential, as well as sensitivity to what concepts and analogies the child will understand.
>
> Throughout the initial interview, remember that a key goal is to develop rapport with the child and parent. Empathy is essential, and appropriate self-disclosure can be helpful. Humor and a fun attitude can also be helpful in reducing anxiety and establishing rapport. With children who are comfortable with it, spend a few minutes without the parent present to ask the "Three Wishes" question (see below) and preview therapy activities that may be involved in further appointments. You can test the child's comfort level with you by asking, "Do you think your Mom (or Dad or both parents) will be OK if she (they) sits and reads by herself in the waiting room while we visit for a few minutes?"
>
> **Good luck and enjoy getting to know your new child client.**

Enhancing the Initial Interview

There are some additional procedures and steps that can enhance the initial interview. They include the following tools:

- Genogram or family map
- "Three Wishes" question
- Miracle Question

Genograms

It is widely recognized that anxiety in children is influenced by both genetics and early life experiences typically within the family environment. When asked if anxiety is innate or learned, I always say, "It's both." An efficient way to capture both of these influences is the genogram, or "family map." Using a variety of symbols that represent the people and events in the life of the child, the genogram can provide a rich and detailed picture of the child in family and historical context. I create a genogram for every case and find it useful in depicting the family dynamics that may need to be addressed as part of child therapy.

A genogram may reveal a correlation between parent and child anxiety when it shows that one parent is a "worrier" just like the child client. Or, I may learn that there were traumatic losses earlier in the life of a child, such as loss of a sibling, parent or pet, or income loss due to a business failure or unemployment of a parent. Or, I may find a history of confusing relationships due to divorce, multiple partners of a parent, out of wedlock pregnancy, adoption and other stresses and adjustments. The genogram is the go-to page in my client record during the first few visits when I want a quick summary of the case. It also helps me remember the names of family members who may accompany the child to the office or who may come up in therapy discussions. In a recent case, the parents appreciated and complimented me on my knowledge of the names and birth order of their child's siblings. The family map provides a window into the "cast of characters" in the life of a child client. I also create a genogram with adult clients for all the same reasons.

The following book is an excellent source of information on how to construct and use genograms:

McGoldrick, M., Gerson, R. and Shellenberger, S. *Genograms: Assessment and Intervention,* 2nd *Ed.* New York: Norton, 1999.

Three Wishes Question

Start with a magic wand, wizard wand or power stick in your hand and ask the following question as you hand it to the client (I keep a collection of magic and wizard wands in my office and sometimes give clients a choice):

"Imagine that in your hand is a real magic wand and you have just been given the power to have any three wishes come true. What would you wish for if you could have three wishes in the world?"

The Three Wishes Question is designed to access the concerns of the client that may not have been verbalized in the presenting problem or by the parent(s). Of course, there is no right or wrong response and I have heard a wide range of wishes, including the following:

- "To not be so worried all the time"
- "To have some direction in life and to have a girlfriend."
- "To be more comfortable around other people."
- "For my mother to be healthy again"
- "For my father to come home."
- "A new Sony PlayStation"
- "An iPhone"
- "For other kids to leave me alone, not bully me."
- "For my mom and dad to get along better, and not get divorced."
- "To win the lottery. I would buy my mother a house."

I am always looking for clues as to the client's motivation level, and I am pleased when one of the wishes hints at a therapy goal. Some of the above referenced wishes speak to motivation and treatment goals: "To not be so worried all the time," "To be more comfortable around other people," and "For other kids to not bully me."

The Miracle Question

The Miracle Question was first published by De Shazer (1985; 1988) as a step in introducing a "solution focus" to therapy. The question is typically asked within the first therapy appointment. I like this intervention because it is one way to develop goals with an anxious child in therapy. The Miracle Question helps us know where we are going in therapy, not just where we are starting. Here is a version you can use with children:

"When you leave my office today, imagine that a miracle occurs in your life and as a result you no longer have the anxiety problem we have been discussing (or name other specific problem). However, the miracle occurs tonight while you are sleeping so you won't know about the change until you wake up tomorrow morning. What will be different, and how will you know you have changed? In the following days and weeks, what new thoughts, feelings or behaviors will you notice?"

Initial Interview Form

Most agencies, clinics and private practitioners use an initial interview form to organize the information to be obtained in the initial interview(s). Some therapists will even use the form during the initial interview as a guide in asking questions and seeking information.

You will notice I continue to use a 5-axes format for the diagnosis, even though this format has been replaced with a single axis diagnosis. I find that the 5-axes format provides for a more detailed diagnostic profile. Note the following abbreviations:

- PP=Presenting Problem
- HX of PP=History of Presenting Problem
- MH RX=Mental Health History
- SX=Symptoms
- D/A=Drug and Alcohol Screening
- MSE=Mental Status Examination
- MED Hx=Medical History
- DX=Diagnosis
- RX=Therapy
- LOS=Length of Stay (predicted time frame or number of sessions)

Patient: _____ Age: _____ Date: _____

Referred By: _____

PP: _____
_____
_____

HX of PP: _____
_____
_____

MH RX:
- _____
- _____
- _____
- _____

● Current SX	

Recent Stress: • _____

• _____

• _____

3 Wishes: 1. _____

2. _____

3. _____

D/A: _____

_____

_____

Special Risk: _____ LOW ____ MED ____ HIGH ____

PSYCHOSOCIAL HX:

• School: _____

_____

• Vocation: _____

_____

• Social: _____

_____

MSE: Affect _____ Control _____

Speech _____ Traits _____

Insight _____ _____

Judgement _____ _____

ATT/CONC _____ _____

Memory _____ _____

Content _____ _____

Med HX: _____
_____
_____

Health: _____

Meds: _____ Prescribed By: _____

    Drug: _____ Dose: _____ A/O _____

    Drug: _____ Dose: _____ A/O _____

    Drug: _____ Dose: _____ A/O _____

    Notes: _____

DX: Axis I _____

       Axis II _____

       Axis III _____

       Axis IV _____

       Axis V _____

RX Goals: 1. _____

              2. _____

              3. _____

              4. _____

              5. _____

RX Modalities: _____
_____

Estimated Los: _____

Notes: _____
_____
_____

Developmental History

The initial clinical interview needs to be supplemented by a development history to get the full picture of present and past functioning. The following developmental history form was created at the Center for Anxiety Disorders and is to be completed by the parent(s) of all clients younger than 18 years of age. You can present the form to parents at the initial interview to be completed by the second interview. The form can also be posted on your web site, if you have one, for parents who want to download it and bring the completed form with them to the initial interview. This step is required by some of the health insurance plans that pay for mental health services. The following is the recommended Developmental History form.

Child Information and Developmental History

Date: _____

Person(s) completing this form: _____ Relationship to child: _____

Child's full name: _____ Birth date: _____ Age: ____

Child's address: _____

Health insurance for child: ☐ Private Company   ☐ Medicaid   ☐ None

PERSON(S) WITH LEGAL CUSTODY OF CHILD

1. ☐ Natural Parent   ☐ Adoptive Parent   ☐ Step Parent   ☐ Foster Parent

Name_____

Address _____ City_____ State_____ Zip_____
(If different from the childs)

Telephone: (H) _____ (W) _____ (Other) _____

Marital/Relationship Status (check one):

☐ Married ☐ Live with Partner ☐ Single ☐ Separated/Divorced ☐ Widowed ☐ Other

Employment Status (Check all that apply):

☐ Employed ☐ Retired ☐ Disabled ☐ Student ☐ Homemaker ☐ Unemployed

If/When Employed, what type of work? _____

Place of work _____

2. ☐ Natural Parent   ☐ Adoptive Parent   ☐ Step Parent   ☐ Foster Parent

Name_____

Address _____ City_____ State_____ Zip_____
(If different from the childs)

Telephone: (H) _____ (W) _____ (Other) _____

Marital/Relationship Status (check one):

☐ Married ☐ Live with Partner ☐ Single ☐ Separated/Divorced ☐ Widowed ☐ Other

Employment Status (Check all that apply):

☐ Employed ☐ Retired ☐ Disabled ☐ Student ☐ Homemaker ☐ Unemployed

If/When employed, what type of work? _____

Place of work _____

Child's natural parents if not listed above: _____

Reason for not living with child: _____

ADULTS AND CHILDREN LIVING IN CHILD'S HOME, IF NOT LISTED ABOVE.

Name	Age	Sex	Relationship to child (step, foster, adoptive, unrelated, etc.)

CHILD'S FULL OR HALF BROTHERS AND SISTERS **NOT** LIVING IN CHILD'S HOME

Name	Age	Sex	Living where?

HOME SETTING

Dates		Location	With whom	Reason for moving	Any problems?
From	To				

RESIDENTIAL PLACEMENTS, INSTITUTIONAL PLACEMENTS, OR FOSTER CARE

Dates		Program Name or Location	Reason for Placement	Problems?
From	To			

SCHOOL

School (name, district, address, phone)	Grade	Age	Teacher

	YES	NO	Describe
Has your child had learning problems?			
Has your child had social problems in school?			
Is your child receiving special help at school?			
Any other school concerns?			

May I call and discuss your child with the current teacher? ☐ Yes ☐ No

What are your concerns about your child?
_____
_____
_____
_____
_____
_____

How long has this difficulty existed?
_____

Have you previously sought help?   ☐ Yes   ☐ No

If yes, where and when?
_____
_____

Do you have any ideas about why your child is having problems now?
_____
_____
_____

CURRENT SYMPTOMS

Symptom	Describe	When did this begin?

Child's Medical History

	Yes	No	Describe
Medical problems during pregnancy?			
Medications during pregnancy?			
Did either parent drink much alcohol during pregnancy?			
Other problems during pregnancy?			
Birth weight and length?			
Was child born premature?			
• If so, how premature?			
Any birth complications or problems?			
Problems with newborn period or infancy?			
Breast-fed?			
• If so, for how long?			
Was or is child allergic to medications, food, etc.?			
Sleep patterns or problems?			

Child's Health
Include all severe illnesses, accidents, operations, handicaps, and repeated medical problems (such as ear infections, headaches, etc.), and other medical conditions.

Condition	Age	Treated by whom?	Consequences?

Medications
List all medications, past and present.

Medication	When first prescribed	Doctor	Effect

Child's Pediatrician

Name_____

Address _____ Telephone _____

Date of last physical exam _____

Results_____

Child's Developmental History

Have you noticed any problems in development? ☐ Yes   ☐ No

Describe

_____

_____

_____

MILESTONES

At what age did the child do each of these? Were any of them difficult or slow to develop?

	Age	Describe
Sat without support		
Crawled		
Walked without holding on		
Helped when being dressed		
Ate with a fork		
Stayed dry all day? All night?		
Didn't soil pants		
Dressed self completely		
Age said first word		
Age said first sentences		
Any speech, hearing, or other impediments/delays?		
Writing		
Reading		
Riding bicycle		
Tying shoes		

Child's Temperament

	YES	NO	Describe
Is your child overactive?			
Does your child have trouble paying attention?			
Does your child have trouble staying with an activity?			
Does your child have fluctuating moods?			
Does your child get frustrated easily?			
Are your child's emotional responses generally unpredictable?			
Does it take your child a long time to warm up to new situations/people?			
Does your child react strongly to physical pain?			
Does your child react strongly to other things?			

Have there been any problems in the following areas?

	YES	NO	Describe
Discipline			
Temper or fighting			
Moods			
Relationship to others			
Sex play			
Other behaviors			

Child's Background

Has anyone in the family had the following? If so, specify relationship to child.

	YES	NO	Relationship	Describe
Neurological disease (seizures, etc.)				
Medical disease (e.g., diabetes, thyroid, heart disease)				
Emotional conditions				
Cognitive or physical delays				
Learning problems				
Behavior problems				
Excessive use of alcohol				
Excessive use of drugs				
Trouble with the law				
Trouble holding a job				
Physical abuse				
Sexual abuse				
Other				

Family Life Stresses

	YES	NO	Explain
Parental separation or divorce			
Family moves			
Recent deaths or losses (within last 3 years)			
Other major family changes			
Has anyone in your family seen a psychologist, psychiatrist, or other mental health care worker?			
Any recent changes/stresses in living situation or family?			

Rate your satisfaction (5 = satisfied, 1 = not satisfied)	1	2	3	4	5	Describe
Your present marriage/relationship						
Your present work situation						
Your present living circumstances						

Summary

Please describe your child's strengths.

_____
_____
_____
_____
_____
_____

What are your child's special skills or talents? List hobbies, sports, recreational, TV, toy preferences, etc.

_____
_____
_____
_____
_____
_____

Please feel free to write anything else you think we should know about your child.

_____
_____
_____
_____
_____
_____
_____
_____

This is a strictly confidential patient medical record. Re-disclosure or transfer is expressly prohibited by law.

Assessment Tools

A clinical interview, such as the one above, coupled with a developmental history, is typically sufficient for the purposes of diagnosis and treatment planning. However, in some cases an additional assessment step is necessary to refine the diagnosis and treatment plan. Some assessment measures require a psychologist license to administer and interpret results, but there are useful anxiety screening tools that are in the public domain and available for use by any mental health professional or other child/adolescent specialists.

Child Anxiety Assessment Tools

Revised Children's Manifest Anxiety Scale-2. Los Angeles: Western Psychological Services, 2011. Tel: (800)-222-2670. This is a 49-item self-report tool (yes/no items) with age norms for children 6-19 that yields four scores for Total Anxiety: Physiological Anxiety, Worry/Oversensitivity, Social Anxiety, and Defensiveness. Also measures for presence of academic stress, test anxiety, peer and family conflicts, and drug problems. Supervision by a licensed psychologist is required to administer and interpret the results of this test.

Multidimensional Anxiety Scale for Children (MASC)-2. San Antonio, TX: The Psychological Corporation (Harcourt Assessment), 2011. Tel: (800) 228-0752. This is a normed 50-item, Likert 4-point scale consisting of self-report and parent report that yields the following scores: Physical Symptoms, Social Anxiety, Harm Avoidance (Perfectionism Subscale, Anxious Coping Subscale), Obsessions and Compulsions, Separation/Panic, Anxiety Disorders, Total Anxiety, and Inconsistency Index. Estimated administration time is 15 minutes. Age range is 8-19. Supervision by a licensed psychologist is required to administer and interpret the results of this test.

Child Behavior Checklist (Teacher Report Form, Parent Report Form, Youth Self-Report Form). Burlington: University of Vermont, 1991. Tel: (802) 264-6432, Fax: (802) 264-6433, email: mail@ASEBA.org web site: www.ASEBA.org This is a behavioral rating tool with age norms that yields scores on several dimensions including Anxiety, Depression, and Attention Problems. Supervision by a licensed psychologist is required to administer and interpret the results of this test.

Social Phobia and Anxiety Inventory for Children (SPAI-C). Evaluates the somatic, cognitive and behavioral aspects of Social Phobia and Anxiety in children between 8-14. Detects social fears that may be related to poor school performance, oppositional behavior or truancy. Self-report form with 26 items and 3rd grade reading level. Supervision by a licensed psychologist is required to administer and interpret the results of this test.

Children's Yale-Brown Obsessive Compulsive Scale (CY-BOCs). Used as a research and clinical assessment tool for ages 6-14, several versions of this scale are widely available online. Use keyword "CY-BOCs." Adult version is Y-Brown OCD Scale (Y-BOCs). This test does not have norms and can be used by any mental health practitioner.

Beck Anxiety Inventory for Youth. Bundled with *Beck Youth Inventories of Emotional and Social Development*. San Antonio, TX: The Psychological Corporation, 1990. Tel: (800) 228-0752. This is a self-report screening tool without age norms and can be used by any mental health practitioner.

Stress Test for Children. Developed and published by Paul Foxman, Ph.D. in his book, *The Worried Child* (2004), this is a screening tool for estimating one of the key sources of anxiety in children. This tool was created on the template of a research-based anxiety test for adults known as the *Life Change Scale (Holmes and Rahe, 1967)*, which conceptualizes stress in terms of the cumulative effect of adjustments or changes. The *Stress Test for Children* is included in Chapter 2 of this book, as part of creating a treatment language and framework to be used with young clients.

Creating a Treatment Framework and Language

Three Ingredients that Cause Anxiety

Based on my clinical work with anxious young clients, as well as keeping up with research on anxiety, I have identified three "ingredients" that account for the development of anxiety disorders. This "Three Ingredient Framework" explains how, why, when and in whom anxiety occurs. With a good grasp on this way of understanding anxiety, you can take the first step in being helpful as a therapist. You can give your child or adolescent clients, and their parents, a reassuring message: that anxiety is understandable, treatable and even has a positive side. After describing this framework, I will provide a child-friendly script that you can use with young clients to explain anxiety and stimulate motivation for therapy.

1. Biological Sensitivity

Approximately 20% of infants are born more sensitive to external and internal stimuli than the average infant (Aron, 2004). In research, these infants are referred as "high reactors." They react strongly to external stimuli such as sounds, lights and temperature, as well as to internal sensations such as tension, fatigue and fluctuations in blood sugar levels. Biological sensitivity refers to this genetic or inborn temperament.

Some examples of biological sensitivity are children who are sensitive to seams and labels in clothes or picky about the taste and texture of food. They may have sleep issues, such as difficulty falling asleep or night waking. In school, they may over-react to the sound of fire alarms or other safety alerts. Highly stimulating environments can overwhelm these sensitive children, and they often require quiet time to recover. Obviously, parents who understand this ingredient are more likely to soothe their children with quiet recovery time, adequate sleep, good diet and nutrition, and physical activity to release tension and stress. *The Highly Sensitive Child* (Aron, 2004) is an excellent resource for parents to help them understand and respond helpfully to their sensitive children.

Research has identified biological sensitivity in infants as young as four months of age (Crockenberg, S. & Leerkes, E., 2006). In one series of studies, infants who reacted more strongly to unfamiliar objects were also more likely to develop an anxiety disorder by the age of 6 when they start first grade in school. On the other hand, these infants were less likely to develop anxiety if the primary care givers modeled coping skills such as refocusing attention away from the unfamiliar objects. "Escape" or "avoidance" of unfamiliar objects was found to increase the likelihood of developing anxiety by school age. The research suggests that specific skills can be taught to children to help them reduce the likelihood of anxiety. In contrast, avoidance perpetuates anxiety and interferes with learning the skills that enable a child—or the adult he or she will become—to gain control over anxiety.

2. Personality Style

The second ingredient in anxiety is a profile of personality traits that are commonly found in anxious children. Many anxious children share these traits in common, and I have termed this pattern the "anxiety personality style." Children with anxiety disorders may not exhibit all of the traits discussed below, but they typically fit the overall pattern by showing a majority of them.

The anxiety-prone child is usually responsible, dependable, and motivated. He or she is typically a good student who is conscientious and strives to do well academically. He or she often shows a need to please adults and peers, and to seek approval and reassurance. As a result, the anxiety-prone child is typically well behaved but often quiet and shy around unfamiliar people.

This type of child also tends to be perfectionistic. He or she wants to do well in everything, and may be unusually disappointed or frustrated with mistakes or imperfect results. Combined with high motivation, this trait often leads to stress even when results or performance are positive. The anxious child may achieve high grades in school but may work relentlessly hard to earn them. Such stress feeds back into the anxiety cycle. In addition, low self-esteem and other negative feelings are associated in many cases with "failing" to be perfect. Perfectionism makes it impossible to relax or take pleasure in accomplishments that do not meet the child's unreasonably high standards.

Paradoxically, perfectionistic children sometimes avoid or procrastinate when they anticipate a difficult task. To avoid feeling inadequate or experiencing "failure," they may shut down and put things off. This is perfectionism disguised as procrastination.

Children with these traits have difficulty relaxing. They are too busy earning positive reinforcement or living up to their own high standards and expectations. When they do relax, it is usually by watching television or participating in other activities that capture their attention. Children with the anxiety personality generally are not lazy or unproductive, although sometimes avoidance or procrastination arising from perfectionism may look to an outsider like "laziness."

Due to their basic sensitivity, children who develop anxiety are readily affected by their surroundings. This includes outside stimuli, such as lights and sounds, as well as the influence of other people. They also tend to be hypersensitive to their own bodily sensations and symptoms.

One of most recognizable anxiety personality patterns is worry. Technically, worry is a cognitive pattern, which can be defined as thoughts about negative events that might happen in the future. Also known as "what-if thoughts," worry is an attempt to feel in control. Unfortunately, the brain's survival center treats every "what-if" thought as something that *will* happen rather than as something that *might* happen. This can activate the fight-flight-or freeze reaction even when no actual danger or threat is present. In children, worry is the primary symptom of generalized anxiety disorder (GAD), as well as a symptom in most of the other anxiety disorders. Besides focusing on the future, worry can also focus on the past, as in ruminating about a mistake or regretting something that has already happened. But worry is usually an excessive preoccupation with an unwanted future event, and the state of nervous anticipation that goes along with it. Worry drains energy, which is why fatigue and somatic complaints are common in worriers. Worry also tends to interfere with a child's ability to relax and to sleep.

Below is a summary of the traits that make up the "anxiety personality style."

- Highly developed sense of responsibility
- Perfectionism
- High expectations

- Oversensitivity to criticism or rejection
- Strong control needs
- Difficulty relaxing
- Tendency to please
- Difficulty with assertiveness
- Frequent worry

Assets and Liabilities of the Anxiety Personality Style:

The traits that make up the anxiety personality have some distinct advantages. Children with this type of personality are high achieving and usually successful in school. They are generally kind, caring, and loyal to their friends, as well as sensitive to the needs and feelings of others. Unless they are shy, such children may even take leadership positions among peers.

On the other hand, children with this personality type tend to feel exceptionally stressed or overwhelmed. While they may do well in school or sports, they may be uncomfortable and driven by a need to please adults and elicit approval from peers. They may take on more than their fair share of responsibilities, only to feel resentful or burdened. In addition, such children take things personally, and their feelings are readily hurt. Due to their need to please others and to avoid rejection, they may not stand up for themselves. As a result, more assertive peers may take advantage of or exploit them. In some cases, they are shy, withdrawn, and lonely. We can think of these as the pitfalls or liabilities of the anxiety personality.

ASSETS	LIABILITIES
Kind, caring, loyal	Above average stress level
Motivated and high achieving	Vulnerable to exploitation
Thoughtful and reflective	Takes things personally
Cooperative	Above average anxiety level

3. Stress Overload

The third ingredient in anxiety is stress. Stress can be considered the "when" factor in anxiety—the condition that activates anxiety in children who are at risk for anxiety by their temperament and personality traits.

As a source of anxiety in children, stress can be any situation that involves unusual demands, strenuous effort, adjustments, or change, and it can be both positive and negative. One research-based measure of stress in adults is the Social Readjustment Rating Scale (Holmes and Rahe, 1967), also known as the Life Change Scale. This screening tool lists 43 life events that are considered stressful, and each item is scored by severity. A total score represents the likelihood of producing physical and emotional symptoms.

The concepts used in the Life Change Scale can be applied to children. The Stress Test for Children (Foxman, 2004) lists the many stresses that can affect children, as well as a scoring system for estimating the likelihood of stress-related symptoms including anxiety. You can use this screening tool to help young clients and their parents recognize their stress sources. This will be an important step in treatment when it comes to teaching stress management skills. The therapeutic message will be that if you can restrict the effects of stress, you can control anxiety.

Sources of Stress in Children

Stress or change	Value	Score
Parent dies	100	
Parents divorce	73	
Parents separate	65	
Separation from parent (placement in foster home, termination of parental rights by authorities, child raised by relatives)	65	
Parent travels for work	63	
Close family member dies	63	
Personal injury, abuse, or illness	53	
Parent remarries	50	
Parent loses job	47	
Separated parents reconcile	45	
Mother starts job outside of home	45	
Change in health of a family member	44	
Mother becomes pregnant	40	
School difficulties	39	
Birth of a sibling	39	
School readjustment (new teacher or class)	39	
Change in family's financial condition	38	
Injury or illness of a close friend	37	
Starts or changes extracurricular activity (e.g., music lessons, sport)	36	
Change in number of fights with sibling(s)	35	
Exposed to violence at school	31	
Theft of personal possessions	30	

Change in responsibilities at home	29	
Older sibling leaves home	29	
Trouble with grandparents	29	
Outstanding personal achievement	28	
Move to another city	26	
Move to another part of town	26	
New pet or loss of pet	25	
Change in personal habits	24	
Trouble with teacher	24	
Change in time with baby-sitter or at day care	20	
Move to new house	20	
Change to new school	20	
Change in play habits	19	
Vacation with family	19	
Change in friends	18	
Attending summer camp	17	
Change in sleeping habits	16	
Change in number of family get-togethers	15	
Change in eating habits	15	
Change in amount of television viewing	13	
Birthday party	12	
Punishment for "not telling the truth"	11	
Child's total score		

Scoring key: Add up all the points for stresses or changes that have occurred during the past year. A score below 150 represents an average stress level. A score between 150 and 300 indicates an above-average stress level. A score above 300 indicates a strong likelihood of health or behavior problems, if no help is provided.

Explaining Anxiety to Children and Parents

The three ingredients framework provides a way to understand in whom, how, when and why anxiety develops. But how can we translate this explanation into child-friendly language?

There are three phases involved in helping young clients and their parents understand anxiety and build a foundation for skill-building therapy. These stages can be labeled:

1. "What's Good about Anxiety:" This phase is designed to instill pride and bolster self-esteem, and to counteract negative views of anxiety.
2. "What You Should Know About Anxiety:" This phase provides a framework for explaining anxiety such as the three-ingredients framework discussed earlier in this chapter.
3. "How would you know if you have anxiety?" This phase introduces the key skills and practices that can help reduce anxiety.

The following child-friendly language can be used to introduce these stages of therapy.

What's Good about Anxiety?

> Anxiety is a normal feeling that everyone has at certain times. Giving a speech in front of other people, taking a test, a sports competition, and other situations produce anxiety for most people. In fact, anxiety at such times can even help by motivating you to practice or prepare in advance so you can do a good job and feel good about it.
>
> But some children and adults have anxiety too much of the time. They worry a lot, or feel anxious at times when it is not necessary. Anxiety gets in the way of enjoying life, and it can make you feel bad about yourself. And yet people with too much anxiety can be successful in school or in their jobs, because they have high standards and they are willing to put time and energy into doing well. In addition, they are usually sensitive to other people's feelings, and they are loyal to their friends. There are many people like this: You are not the only one.
>
> In my experience as a psychologist, children with anxiety are intelligent, imaginative and creative. They tend to have talents in art, music, writing, sports and other areas. Such children are also likeable, friendly, and easy to get along with. What amazes me is how children who are anxious can be so nice and friendly, even when they are so nervous inside. Sometimes no one else knows how uncomfortable you are inside. If you are an anxious child, do not feel bad or get down on yourself. You have many positive qualities, and I believe the world would be a better place if there were more people like you. Best of all, you can change many of the anxious feelings and behaviors, and you can reach your potential as a person. Visiting with a therapist is one step you can take to feel better and enjoy life more.

What You Should Know about Anxiety

> One of the best ways to understand anxiety is to imagine that you are a small animal, say a rabbit, living in nature. In the animal world there is a system of predators and prey, and animals know instinctively whether they are safe or in danger. When a vulnerable animal is threatened, it senses danger and reacts with survival behavior, such as hiding, until it is safe again. When it is safe, the animal relaxes and resumes normal activities.

In the world of people, we sometimes feel unsafe even though there is no danger. We perceive danger when it does not actually exist. And when we feel this way, we react with survival behaviors, such as avoiding things, wanting to hide, or getting revved up in our bodies. When there is no real danger, we call this survival reaction "anxiety." High stress can also cause the survival reaction, and it is one of the biggest reasons for anxiety. On the following page, you will learn how to know when your stress is high, as well as what you can do to bring it down and relax.

Another reason for anxiety is emotional or physical trauma. A trauma is an extreme event that is not a normal part of life. Here is a list of some traumas that can happen to children:

- Parents separate or get divorced
- A serious injury or being hurt by another person
- Being touched in private parts of your body by another person
- Being embarrassed in front of other people
- Having a fire in your house
- Having a hurricane or tornado damage your house
- A car accident
- Losing a parent or a friend
- Having a serious illness, or going to the hospital
- Seeing violence on television or in real life

Some children are more likely than others to develop anxiety under stress or when a trauma happens to them. They are born with a sensitive temperament, and they tend to react more strongly to things. For example, such children may be picky about the food they eat because they react strongly to certain foods.

Children who become anxious also have a certain type of personality. For example, they often try too hard to please other people, and they sometimes say "yes" when they feel "no" because they don't want to upset other people or make them angry. They try to do everything perfectly, and they get upset when they make mistakes. They can be too serious and have difficulty playing or relaxing. They may worry a lot and have trouble enjoying life.

But children do not automatically feel anxious just because they are sensitive or have this type of personality. Anxiety comes when these two things are combined with too much stress or with a traumatic event. We already talked about traumas that can happen to children.

What about stress?

Stress can consist of too many changes, or too many things happening all at once. Sometimes stress builds up over a period of a few months and catches us by surprise. Stress can consist of positive things as well as negative things. Any change or adjustment can be stressful, especially when there are too many things happening in a short period of time. There is a children's stress scale that we can use to estimate your stress level.

Some of the stresses on the stress test are:

- Moving to another city or neighborhood
- Changing teachers or going to a new school
- Getting a new pet, or losing a pet
- Birth of a sibling
- Parent losing a job
- More fights with a brother or sister
- Problems in school
- Theft of a personal possession
- Going to summer camp

How Would You Know If You Have Anxiety?

Most of the time, we know when we are anxious because certain things happen inside us. For example, we probably feel anxious if we have trouble going to sleep at night or if we worry a lot. Here are some clues about anxiety:

- Sudden body reactions (racing heart, difficulty breathing, nervous stomach)
- Frequent worry
- Difficulty falling asleep, or waking up in the middle of the night
- Wanting to avoid school or social situations
- Feeling nervous when you remember something bad that happened
- Having unwanted or repetitive thoughts
- Urges to do things that waste time or that you don't want to do

Another important thing to know is that you can control anxiety, and you can even prevent it by doing certain things on a regular basis. These are the skills that we will focus on in our work together.

As your counselor, my job is to help you learn these skills with the goal of helping you be successful in making anxiety go away.

The three-ingredients framework informs us as to the recommendations, skills and interventions that we will need to incorporate into therapy with anxious children. The three-ingredients framework suggests that the following steps are necessary for effective treatment:

- Behavioral recommendations to address biological sensitivity: this means addressing sleep, diet/nutrition, physical activity and managing children's media exposure
- Teaching and encouraging the practice of stress management skills
- Controlling the personality traits that contribute to anxiety, these include perfectionism, worry, and difficulty relaxing

Regardless of the particular anxiety condition or disorder, every case would benefit from these basic interventions.

Foundation Skills For Managing Anxiety

As you move beyond assessment and treatment planning, it is appropriate to suggest, teach and encourage practices that reduce stress and resulting anxiety. Your therapy goal in this stage is to draw from a repertoire of skills and discover the one or two procedures that work for each client, and then to motivate regular practice.

In this chapter, you will find a collection of self-regulation practices beginning with behavioral health suggestions and stress management techniques that include key relaxation skills.

Based on the framework for understanding anxiety that is discussed in Chapter 2, the first focus of therapy should be on four behavioral health recommendations, sleep, diet and nutrition, exercise and movement and managing media exposure

Sleep

The American Academy of Pediatrics (AAP) recommends 9.5 hours of sleep per night for teens and 10-11 hours of sleep per night for children between the ages of 7-12. However, surveys of youth sleep patterns reveal that many children and adolescents do not get the recommended number of hours of sleep. A survey of high school students, for example, found that 90% report getting no more than 6 hours of sleep on school nights. Furthermore, 92% reported that they rarely get a good night's sleep during the school week. This means that most teens are functioning on a 15-hour sleep deficit per school week.

You can help motivate child and adolescent clients to schedule enough sleep by "working backwards" with time management. Begin by asking what time the client needs to be in school at the start of the day. Then ask how much time is needed to get to school, followed by how much time is needed before leaving the house starting with getting out of bed, including washing, dressing, and eating breakfast. Then ask how much time it takes to get from waking up to getting out of bed, followed by how many hours of sleep are recommended for children or adolescents their age. Continue the line of questioning until it becomes clear what time they need to start getting ready for bed the evening before, to include preparing for sleep and falling asleep. Many children will be surprised to do the math and realize that an appropriate bedtime is much earlier than they believed.

For young people who report difficulty falling asleep, there are some behavioral health recommendations for improving sleep. Here is a handout for addressing sleep issues such as insomnia and night waking:

Sleep Recommendations

- Relaxing ambiance at nighttime (e.g. dim lighting)
- Establish a consistent sleep cycle 7 days a week
- Make sleep a priority and avoid temptation to stay up late
- No television within one hour of sleep (too stimulating)
- Warm bath (or foot bath): 92-970 F (see also aromatherapy below)
- Avoid daytime naps if difficulty falling asleep at night
- Use bed only for sleep
- Quality sleep requires a good mattress that provides comfort and support
- Regular exercise aids sleep (but not within 2 hours of bedtime)
- Relaxing activity (reading, gentle music, breathing exercise) before bedtime
- If wake up and can't resume sleep, get up and do something (go to bathroom, drink water or herb tea, read) until fatigue induces sleep
- Food considerations: Avoid over-eating and stimulants (chocolate, sodas, black tea, coffee ice cream or chemical additives that increase heart rate) before bed. "Good foods" for sleep include tea with chamomile (e.g. "Sleepytime Tea") and "Horlick's Hot Malted Milk" (supported by research)
- Aromatherapy: Some essential oils, such as lavender, are considered calming and can be added in the amount of 6 drops to a warm bath to induce relaxation and sleep.
- Massage: Gentle stroking and kneading of body or just feet using massage oil with lavender and chamomile

DISCLAIMER: This list of suggestions is for your interest only and is not intended to be prescriptive for individuals. Information is compiled from a variety of sources. Discuss all treatments with your personal health care professional.

Diet and Nutrition

There are at least two issues to be addressed regarding diet and nutrition: **when** we eat and **what** we eat. Let's start with **when**. Dieticians suggest the healthiest way to eat is small meals 4-5 times each day. This pattern can be especially helpful for biologically sensitive children and teens. In some cases this might mean re-examining what constitutes a meal. Perhaps healthy snacks such as yogurt and fruit, soup and crackers, a sandwich, or cheese and crackers could be used to keep blood sugar and energy more consistent between larger, cooked meals.

What we eat is the second issue. A starting point is to distinguish between healthy, natural and whole foods as compared to refined, sugared and processed foods. Of course, improving the quality of food requires participation of parents who typically do the grocery shopping. It might be helpful to introduce the concept of "good foods and bad foods for anxiety." Here is some child-friendly language to use in a discussion of diet and nutrition with young clients:

Child Friendly Language for Diet and Nutrition Recommendations

Some foods can make anxiety worse, and some foods can help you control anxiety. Remember that some children have a special sensitivity that makes them more likely to have anxiety. The same sensitivity can also influence your reaction to foods, and it is important to know which are the good foods and the bad foods for anxiety. Foods that contain caffeine are not good for anxiety. Caffeine is a substance that speeds up your nervous system, and some people like it because it helps them feel more awake or alert when they are tired. But if you have anxiety you are already alert and nervous: You don't need any more chemicals to wake up. In fact, foods with caffeine will make you more anxious. What foods contain caffeine? Many sodas contain caffeine, and they should be eliminated from your diet. Also, coffee, hot chocolate, and non-herbal teas contain caffeine. If you like chocolate, you can have a small amount as a treat after you eat a good meal. That way, the effect of the caffeine will be less sudden. Sugared foods might also make you more nervous. These include cakes, candies, ice cream, cookies, sweet rolls, sweetened cereals, fruit punch, and sugary sodas (even those that are caffeine-free, such as Sprite). Like many children, you probably like these foods. My suggestion is that you have them only a few times each week, and it would best to eat them as a dessert after a meal rather than by themselves in between meals.

The best foods are fruits, vegetables, protein, and grains (good bread, spaghetti and other noodles, non-sugared cereals, and rice). These foods will provide good nutrition needed for growth, and they will not make you feel nervous. They will also help to keep your energy up so you don't feel weak and anxious. Some other suggestions are to avoid eating too much at one time because that makes you feel tired and slow. It is better to have good food snacks spread throughout the day when you are hungry. Good food snacks include apples, raisins, peanut butter and crackers, popcorn, and cheese and crackers. Don't forget to drink enough water. Water is the best drink, and you need more than you think. You could get headaches or other body reactions if you don't drink enough water. The best way to remember to drink enough water is to carry a water bottle around with you. That way, you will see it and remember to drink.

List of Good Foods and Bad Foods for Anxiety

Good Foods

Fruits: All fresh fruits (avoid fruits canned in heavy syrup) – Fruit rollups

Vegetables: Raw or cooked, and salads

Proteins: Meats, fish, poultry, peanut butter, beans

Grains: Good bread, pasta (spaghetti, noodles, macaroni), rice, whole wheat pizza

Dairy: Milk (low fat), cheese, yogurt (low fat)

Snacks: Crackers, pretzels, popcorn, rice cakes, trail mix, raw vegetables (e.g., carrots), fresh fruit, protein bars

Water: Drink plenty of water every day (carry a water bottle to help you remember)

Bad Foods

Sugary foods: Cakes, cookies, candy, fruit punch, sweet rolls, ice cream, high-fat foods with sugar

Caffeine: Sodas (most but not all), energy drinks, coffee, hot chocolate, non-herbal teas

Eating dinner is a good way for you and your family to spend time together. Try slowing down and relaxing when you eat. This will help prevent eating too much, and it will aid in the digestion of your food. Eating more slowly also allows you to visit and talk about things, such as how your day went and plans for the future.

Exercise and Movement

Our bodies were designed to move, as evidenced by the joints and muscles that allow us to walk, run, jump and perform countless physical activities. It is common knowledge that exercise is essential for physical health and well-being. But movement is also important for anxiety reduction. We can relax our minds through the improved breathing that comes from exercise. We can relieve mental stress as well as physical tension through movement and exercise. Exercise and movement also has a synergistic effect on improving sleep quality, which is typically compromised by worry and anxiety. Movement is an essential behavioral health recommendation for our sensitive and anxious young clients.

Movement does not have to be vigorous to be beneficial; we can use mindfulness walking, movement meditations or practice yoga for anxiety reduction. Some therapists who work with young people find that walking together during therapy sessions can facilitate communication as well as model the mental and physical benefits of movement. Walking side by side seems to reduce the intensity of eye-to-eye contact, "loosen up" the mind, and contribute to more authentic communication.

Exercise and movement *outdoors* has added benefits for anxiety reduction. Exposure to the rhythms of nature—light and dark cycles, seasonal cycles, gentle breezes—help to reset and calm our internal rhythms. We have many internal rhythms, such as sleep, digestive, and metabolic patterns, that are calmed and regulated by exposure to nature.

Each client should be encouraged to do something physical, preferably outdoors, every day. This is now being referred to as a daily "green hour." Spending time outdoors is the essence of *recreation*, which literally means to "*recreate*" or "*restore*" oneself. The research on exposure to nature as a powerful form of therapy is detailed in a book entitled, *Last Child in the Woods: Saving Our Children from Nature Deficit Disorder* (Louv, 2008). The book has galvanized an international "Leave No Child Inside" movement that recognizes a generation of children so plugged into electronic diversions that it has lost its connection to the natural world.

In guiding your clients to design a personal stress management program, include exercise and movement. Generally speaking there are three components to a complete exercise and movement program:

- Cardiovascular exercise
- Strength training
- Stretching and flexibility training

These components can be varied based on the season, weather, resources available and other conditions that need to be accommodated. They can also be cycled with the other stress management practices and activities discussed in this chapter. The message should be to engage in at least one stress reducing activity every day. Clients who tell you they have no time for exercise are really saying they have not made a priority of self-care. You can help motivate clients by focusing on the desired outcome of these recommended activities. Help them connect the dots between these recommendations and their goals for therapy.

Managing Children's Media Exposure

This stress management component is related to the sleep deficit plaguing children and adolescents today. Research on the effects of over-exposure to the "blue light" emitted by electronic screens—smart phones, video screens, computers and LED televisions—is showing inhibiting effects on the human brain's production of the sleep-promoting hormone, melatonin. The AAP reports that children and adolescents spend an average of 7 hours per day exposed to electronic screens. Based on recommendations by the AAP, children and adolescents should turn off all electronic screens one hour before bedtime. This, of course, requires parents to be onboard with the recommendation.

In addition to the issue of brain-stimulating "blue light," the violent content of many forms of media should be addressed. For example, the American Psychological Association (APA) reports that children who watch 2 or more hours of television per day (average is 3-4 hours/day) are likely to experience three negative effects, the first of which is a direct link to anxiety.

- More fear and anxiety
- More aggressive behavior
- Lower emotional empathy

Intense violence is everywhere in the media, including video games (some branches of the U.S. military teach soldiers how to kill using commercial video games), movies, television and some youth oriented music. Even Saturday morning cartoons have been found to include an average of 46 violent acts per hour. To address both the light and the content issues in children's use of media, the AAP has issued some specific recommendations.

- Turn off all electronic screens 1 hour before bedtime

- Establish "screen-free" zones at home (e.g. no televisions, computers or video games in children's bedrooms)

- Turn off the TV during dinner
- Limit entertainment to high-quality content for 1-2 hours per day
- Children should spend time on outdoor play, reading, hobbies, and using their imaginations in free play
- Avoid television and entertainment media for infants and children under age 2

As a therapist, you can share with parents the recommendations of the AAP and advise an experiment: see what happens as a result of the implementing the suggested limit on media exposure for a reasonable time period, such as a week or 10 days. To conduct this experiment, parents will also need to manage their own media diet and turn off their electronic screens an hour before bedtime.

Here are some resources for managing children's media exposure:

Resources for Managing Children's Media Exposure

www.aap.org Web site of the American Academy of Pediatrics. Offers guidelines on appropriate media for children. Select "Children's Health Topics," such as "Internet/Media Use."

www.apa.org Web site of the American Psychological Association. Select "Kids and the Media" for information on effects of television and media on children.

www.cmch.tv Web site of the Center on Media and Child Health that contains useful suggestions and tips for parents to manage children's media exposure.

www.commonsensemedia.org One-stop web site for reviews and ratings of movies, television and video games for content and age-appropriateness.

www.ncta.com Web site of The National Cable and Telecommunications Association. Offers personalized instructions on how to configure parental controls on TV and cable equipment.

www.esrb.org/ratings Videogame rating system of the Entertainment Software Rating Board.

www.kff.org Web site of the Kaiser Family Foundation, dedicated to providing information on health care issues to professionals and the general public. See article entitled "The Effects of Electronic Media on Children Ages Zero to Six: A History of Research."

www.kid-in-mind.com Detailed movie ratings in three content areas: violence/gore, profanity, sex/nudity

www.mpaa.org Movie rating system by the Motion Picture Association of America.

www.tvguidelines.org Television program rating system by the TV Parental Guidelines Monitoring Board. Free download of brochure, "Navigating Your Way through the TV Parental Guidelines and V-Chip."

Beyond Behavioral Health

Beyond behavioral health, when you work with children and adolescents to create a personal stress management program, you are addressing a key trigger for anxiety (see Chapter 2). Some of the options for stress management are also necessary for diagnosis-specific therapy interventions that will be discussed in Chapter 4. For example, skill in relaxation and self-calming is necessary for exposure therapy that will be recommended for separation anxiety disorder, specific phobias, social anxiety disorder, panic disorder and obsessive-compulsive disorders (including hair pulling and skin picking).

Fortunately, there are many options from which to choose based on your sense of what would be most appropriate for each client. What follows below are some of the techniques you can introduce, each accompanied by an instruction sheet that you can give to your clients or their parents depending on age and motivation. Once again, your challenge is to match each client with an appropriate self-regulation procedure and encourage regular practice.

To encourage regular practice, you can use sports or other analogies. For example, a 9-year old boy who loved basketball was asked, "When would it be best to practice your foul shots?" He immediately recognized that practice before competitive games is best so that accuracy is more likely when it really counts. You can also inquire about skills that a child has already acquired, such as playing a musical instrument, computer use, etc. Then follow up by pointing out that proficiency is the result of practice, beginning with mistakes that provide feedback about what to improve until proficiency is attained.

3-S Process for Stress Management

As stress is one of the triggers for anxiety, stress management skills can go a long way in reducing anxiety. For this purpose, I have developed the "3-S Process for Stress Management." Many skills and practices will be included, and your task as therapist is to match each client with an appropriate stress management practice. Each of the three steps for teaching stress management skills to young people can be designated by a word that begins with the letter, S:

1. Symptoms
2. Sources
3. Solutions

Step 1: Symptoms

The first of the three stress management steps consists of identifying the specific stress symptoms in a child or adolescent. Frequently, the symptoms in a young person are the presenting problems or reason for the therapy referral. Alternative names for "symptoms" are "signals" or "signs" of stress, also "s" words.

Symptoms generally fall into three groups. Below are some examples of symptoms in each group.

1. **Mood**
   - Negative attitude
   - Irritability
   - Depression
   - Anxiety

2. **Behavior**
   - Aggression
   - Withdrawal/avoidance

3. **Somatic**
   - Sleep disturbance
   - Headaches
   - Restlessness
   - Grinding teeth
   - Increased heart rate
   - Cold/sweaty hands
   - Breathing difficulty
   - Muscle tension
   - Fatigue/low energy

Step 2: Sources

The sources of stress vary widely but can also be classified into three groups:

1. Family
2. School
3. Media

The family sources are itemized on the Stress Test for Children, found in Chapter 2. Some, like the role of divorce, need to be addressed as part of your ongoing relationship with the child client. In such cases, the treatment plan might involve the parents directly by scheduling regular or periodic parent conferences. The goal of these sessions is to influence parents to be more sensitive to their child's needs for structure, predictability and emotional support. With older adolescents on the threshold of leaving home for college, the focus might more appropriately be on advising them on how to negotiate with their parents regarding their needs. Focusing on the older adolescent's emerging autonomy is often more productive and developmentally appropriate than trying to change the parents.

From a family systems perspective, a child's or adolescent's symptoms may reflect a problem on the part of the parents. In this framework, the child or adolescent client is the "identified patient" who is sent by the parents to therapy as the person who needs to be "fixed." This takes the pressure off the parents who, in many cases, are the source of the child's symptoms. These dynamics are usually "unconscious" and not recognized by the client or parents. There may even be a system of denial about the source of the problem.

In one case, for example, an anxious 17-year old girl revealed to her therapist that she had been cutting herself, and she knew this high-risk behavior would need to be reported to her parents. In fact, she also showed the therapist a letter that she had addressed but not given to her parents. The letter was a poignant description of the parents' daily alcohol drinking pattern, including frequent situations where she would find her mother and father passed out in the house. The therapist recognized that her client's self-harm behavior was a call to get help for her parents' alcohol addiction and their inability to show concern for the daughter's loneliness and anxiety. In a skilled session with the parents, the therapist learned that the parents were coping with two significant stresses that were interfering with their parenting: a business loss and an extra-marital affair. The outcome of the session was that the parents agreed to follow up with alcoholism treatment and pursue counseling to save their marriage. It was clear in this case that the adolescent client was the "identified patient" whose symptoms were, in part, an unconscious call to get help for the parents.

Step 3: Solutions

The third step in this approach to stress management consists of teaching skills and encouraging activities that reduce stress. Such interventions counteract anxiety by controlling the stress factor, or what could be called the "when factor" in anxiety. The following stress management interventions are addressed below:

- The Magic Word
- Breathing Games and Practices
- Time Management
- Mindfulness Skills
- Yoga
- Meditation for Preschool Children
- Martial Arts
- Flow activities

The Magic Word

This stress management intervention is based on research by a cardiologist, Herbert Benson, M.D., who has spent over 40 years researching the benefits of transcendental meditation. Benson (1984) used the term Relaxation Response in reference to a deep state of relaxation—deeper than sleep—with many physical and cognitive benefits.

Benson's research led to the following conclusion:

> We all have an. . . *"inborn capacity to enter a special state characterized by lowered heart rate, decreased rate of breathing, lowered blood pressure, slower brain waves, anti-inflammatory changes, anti-oxidation processes. This state reduces anxiety, depression, insomnia. . ..In this relatively peaceful condition, the individual's mental patterns change so that he breaks free of what I call worry cycles. These are unproductive (neural) grooves or circuits that cause the mind to play over and over again, almost involuntary, the same anxieties or uncreative, health-impairing thoughts."* (Benson, 1984, p. 5)

In the early phase of his research, Benson used the traditional transcendental meditation instructions, which consisted of four steps. In the most recent version, he found that two simple steps could elicit the anti-anxiety state. The two-step instructions are conceptually simple enough to be comprehended even by young children. I usually introduce it as *The Magic Word* or *The Special Word* technique. Below is an instruction sheet for teaching this skill to children and adolescents. You will note that this is a classical conditioning practice whose goal is to pair a "magic" or "special" word with a relaxed state. Through repeated practice, simply thinking about or repeating the word can have the power to induce a relaxed state.

The Magic Word or Special Word technique also improves attention, focus and concentration, all of which can be impaired by anxiety. This technique can also be used as an intervention for attention deficit disorder.

Magic Word Instructions For Children

The Magic Word technique consists of two steps practiced once or twice each day. Length of practice should be based on age, attention span, emotional maturity, motivation and other factors. Two to five minutes once per day would be appropriate for young children and length of time can be extended up to 20 minutes two times per day for adults.

These are the two steps:

1. Repetition of a special word or phrase that is synchronized with slow breathing
2. Refocus on the repetition whenever other thoughts intrude

Research shows that the effectiveness of this technique is enhanced when the repeated word or phrase has personal meaning. Therefore, collaborate with the child in selecting a "Magic Word" or phrase.

A two-syllable word is easiest for young children to synchronize with breathing. The first half of the word or phrase is repeated silently during the in-breath and the second half is repeated during the out-breath. Some examples are:

- Re-laxed
- Be calm
- Feel good
- Stay calm
- Peace-full
- O-kay
- Calm down
- Hap-py
- Be strong
- I can
- Be cool

Breathing Games and Practices

Most relaxation practices emphasize deep and slow breathing. We can voluntarily control the respiratory system, which, in turn, has a calming effect on other organ systems such as the cardiovascular and neuromuscular systems. In other words, deep and slow breathing is the key to controlling the body. Furthermore, as Benson's research (1984) found, a relaxed body is associated with a calm mind. A calm mind counteracts worry, and improves learning and memory.

There are many breathing games and practices that are appropriate and effective with children. These can range from blowing a long stream of bubbles, pretending to use the breath to cool a bowl of hot soup and other breathing techniques. Below are the instructions for some child-friendly breathing practices.

Breathing Practices for Children

The respiratory system has a regulating effect on all our body systems (heart, nerves, muscles, digestion). We can learn to relax and control our whole body by practicing these breathing exercises.

Balloon Breathing

Sit up straight, place one hand over your stomach and concentrate on your breathing. Feel how your stomach fills up as you breathe in and goes down as you breathe out. Imagine a balloon inside your stomach that fills itself with air as you inhale and empties itself of air as you exhale. Try to feel the balloon with your hand. Notice your whole body relaxing, as your breathing becomes deep and full. Practice this exercise for about one minute and use this technique whenever you feel anxious.

Alternate instructions for preschool children and kindergarteners: "Lie on your back and place a teddy bear or other stuffed animal on your stomach. Watch the animal as you breathe and try to make it move up and down as you breathe in and out."

Breathing With Sounds

This exercise can be done with children in a group or individually. Inhale deeply and make a soft sound, such as AH, HA, O, OO or MMM, as you exhale. You can also use animal noises. In a group, select a leader to choose the sound and have the others copy the sound. A variation of this exercise is to make the sound last as long as possible, followed by a deep, full inhalation.

Breathing By Numbers

Calming Breath: For this breathing practice, try to make your in-breath and out-breath equal in time. Do this by counting slowly (one second for each count) as you breathe in and then counting for the same amount of time as you breathe out. Practice this breathing exercise for about two minutes once or twice each day, and use it whenever you feel tense or anxious.

Counting Breath: This exercise can be introduced as a method of relaxation involving counting, where each count represents one second. Each in-breath is the same for the count of 2, and each out-breath increases by 2, as follows:

In 2—Out 2   In 2—Out 8

In 2—Out 4   In 2—Out 10

In 2—Out 6

Time Management

Time management and personal organization are important skills for the young person whose anxiety is associated with falling behind in school, losing track of details or belongings, and generally feeling out of control. What system can be used with children and adolescents to help them get in control of their lives?

The approach to time and life management by Covey (1998; 2008) was developed specifically for children as well as adults. There are several important concepts and strategies that I have used effectively with young people:

- Know what's important. Have your client give some thought to what Covey calls "values" or what could also be referred to as "priorities." You can discuss this with your clients by asking the question, "What is important to you? Your health? Your grades in school?
- Spend the most time on the things that are most important. Encourage your clients to put time into those things that matter most.
- Do the most important things first. Your clients should keep their priorities in mind when they plan their time, and start with the most important things.

Our daily activities can be listed on a chart with four quadrants based on two axes: importance and urgency. Importance refers to the relative importance of daily activities and tasks, and urgency refers to the degree to which activities and tasks have external deadlines or accountability. Research finds that people who rate themselves high on life satisfaction spend time on a regular basis engaged in activities that are important to them but for which there is little external accountability (Covey, Merrill and Merrill, 1994). These are called "Quadrant 2" activities because on a chart they fall into the quadrant that represents what is important to an individual person but where there is no external deadline or accountability (unless parents are making these activities important). Examples would include self-health practices (exercise, getting enough sleep, eating well) as well as hobbies and flow activities (see "Flow" in this chapter). The research was done with adults but it seems reasonable to assume the findings would apply to children and adolescents.

You can use the next exercise to help your clients manage their time based on what is important to them. At the end of any given day, the child or adolescent client lists key activities and tasks from the day in the appropriate quadrant and notices what has been accomplished as well as what sources of motivation were involved.

Time Management Exercise (Quadrants)

Client name: _____   Today's date: _____

	URGENT **QUADRANT 1**	NOT URGENT **QUADRANT 2**
HIGHER IMPORTANCE		

	QUADRANT 3	**QUADRANT 4**
LOWER IMPORTANCE		

Copyright © 2017 Paul Foxman. *The Clinician's Guide To Anxiety Disorders In Kids and Teens.* All rights reserved.

QUADRANT KEY:

1. Important/Urgent: These are "must-do" items which are important to you as well as urgent to someone else. Examples include doing homework, chores, etc.
2. **Important/Not Urgent: These are items of importance to you, such as your health, family relationships, and personal goals, but they are not accountable to anyone else. Successful people spend some time in Quadrant 2 on a daily basis.**
3. Not Important/Urgent: These are items that are not important to you, but are needed by others. Learn how to do these efficiently so you will have more time for things that are important to you.
4. Not Important/Not Urgent: Discontinue doing things that are not important to you or anyone else. Successful people spend less than 1% of time in this quadrant.

A time management exercise that can be used with teens to help with life satisfaction is called the Life Balance Exercise. The 2-step therapy activity focuses on how much time is spent in six life areas or domains, followed by an opportunity to reallocate time to improve life satisfaction. Although the instructions are self-explanatory, it is recommended that you discuss with your adolescent client the purpose of the exercise and how it fits with time management skills.

Life Balance Exercise (Adolescent)

LIFE DOMAINS:

1. School
2. Family
3. Self Care (e.g. exercise/ recreation, reading, hobbies, personally meaningful activities)
4. Social
5. Chores
6. Spiritual (e.g. volunteering, community service, meditation)

In the circle below, draw "slices of pie" sections representing the percentage of time you **NOW** spend in each of the six life domains (use above list of life domains for reference).

In the circle below, draw sections showing how you could reallocate your time to **IMPROVE** your life balance.

Yoga for Children

Yoga is an empirically based practice for calming and relaxation, and there are some child-friendly poses that are well suited for this purpose. Yoga can be helpful in reducing anxiety by calming the nervous system. Yoga also centers the mind as it calms the physical body. Yoga combines breathing and movement to relax muscles, tendons, and internal organs. In addition, yoga increases oxygenation of the blood, activates stretch receptors throughout the body, and encourages physical patterning that is generally calm and rhythmic.

A growing amount of mind-body and brain-based research shows that when children learn yoga, they become more present, empowered to manage their emotions and more successful in school life (see web sites for supporting research and articles in the resource list below in this section). The benefits of yoga including the following:

- Reduces anxiety
- Relieves tension and stress
- Calms and clears the mind
- Brings children into the present moment
- Improves concentration focus, attention span and memory
- Promotes creative thinking
- Improves emotional self-regulation
- Increases self-awareness

Yoga is appealing to young people because there are many fun and interesting poses. The poses draw from animals, nature and everyday objects. Here are some child-friendly animal poses, beginning with standing postures that flow naturally to sitting and lying down.

Individual Poses:
- Mountain
- Rag Doll
- Giraffe
- Eagle
- Tree
- Downward Dog/Wag Your Tail
- Dolphins/Spouting Dolphin
- Happy Cat
- Scared Cat

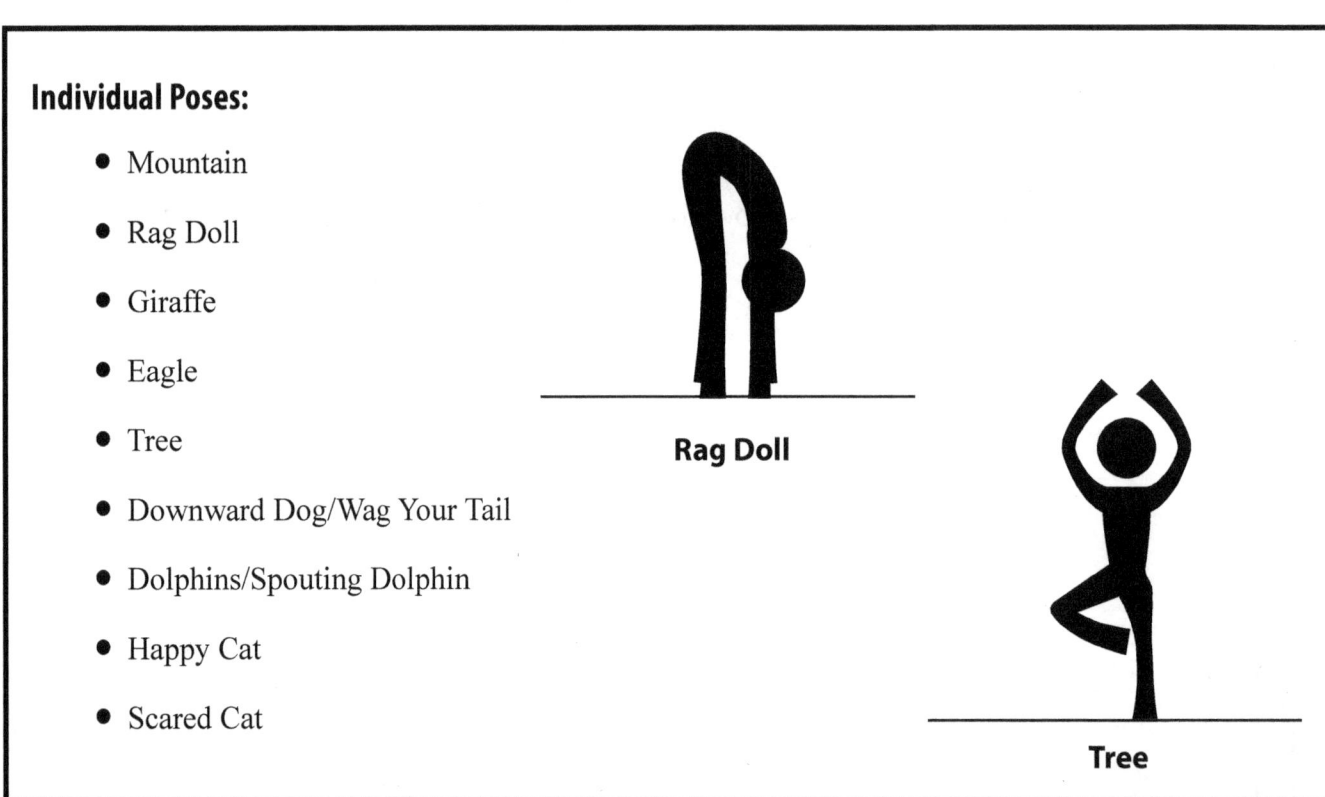

- Spider
- Boat/Challenging Boat
- Camel
- Child's Pose
- Cobra
- Upward Facing Dog
- Plow
- Candle
- Bridge
- Fish
- Crocodile

Spider

Camel

Plow

Upward Facing Dog

Bridge

Candle

In addition to individual yoga postures, there are also some partner poses that can be used to address social anxiety and to promote trust, negotiation skills, teamwork and communication skills. Partner poses can be done with peers or family members including parents. Some examples of partner poses are:

Partner Poses:

- Elevator
- Lizard on a Rock
- Double Dog
- Park Bench
- Partner Sailboat
- Submarine

There are even family and group yoga games that are appropriate for enhancing communication, fitness and community. Here are some examples:

- **Guess the pose:** each person takes a turn at a pose and the group must guess the pose
- **Pose tag:** one person is chosen as "It" and after tagging the next "It" tells that person what pose to perform
- **Create-a-Pose:** each person in the family or group makes up a new pose, gives it a name and performs it for the group

Finally, yoga is also an excellent practice for therapists, counselors, educators and others who work professionally with people. Yoga can help counteract the occupational hazards of our work, including:

- Physical tension and postural misalignment from extended periods of sitting
- Emotional drain from client needs
- Mental overload from processing so much client information
- Eye strain from sustained focus on body language and visual cues

I find the following sequence of poses to be an effective antidote for our occupational stress:

- **Standing postures:** sun salutation, backwards bends, forward hanging bends, lateral bends
- **Floor work:** forward reach to toes, half plow, full plow, bridge, fish, shoulder stand, headstand, arm rotations (shoulder stretch)
- **Sitting:** neck rolls, eye exercises, breathing exercises

There are many resources for introducing yoga into therapy with children and adolescents. These include books, DVDs, classes, YouTube videos and "Yoga Education" programs used in schools. If you are interested in incorporating yoga into your work, one option is to take a personal interest and learn some yoga poses. The best way to teach yoga is to demonstrate the poses and do them with your clients. Research shows that experiential learning is more effective that auditory and visual learning.

Here are some resources for incorporating yoga into your work with children and adolescents:

Yoga for Children Resources

BOOKS:

Baptiste, B. *My Daddy is a Pretzel: Yoga for Parents and Children.* Cambridge, MA: Barefoot Books, 2004.

Bersma, D. *Yoga Games for Children.* Alameda, CA: Hunter House, 2003.

Flynn, L. *Yoga for Children: 200+ Yoga Poses, Breathing Exercises, and Meditations for Healthier, Happier, More Resilient Children.* Avon, MA: Adams Media, 2013.

Lidell, L. *The Sivananda Companion to Yoga.* New York: Simon and Schuster, 1983.

Purperhart, H. *The Yoga Adventure for Children: Playing, Dancing, Moving, Breathing, Relaxing.* Alameda, CA: Hunter House, 2006.

Stewart, M. *Yoga for Children.* New York: Fireside, 1992.

WEB SITES:

Childlightyoga.com

cosmickidsyoga.com

Thekidsyogaresource.com

yoga4classrooms.com

Mindfulness Skills for Children and Adolescents

Mindfulness can be defined as follows: "Awareness of present experience without judgment." Mindfulness is a state of mind and a way of being in daily life that involves full attention to and awareness of what we are doing from moment to moment. Mindfulness is the opposite of multi-tasking: it is the process of being fully engaged in each activity. Mindfulness is also a term used to describe the various practices that cultivate this state of mind. There are many such activities that are appropriate, office friendly and fun for children.

The mindfulness practice that I find most effective with children is called "savoring." While any number of activities can be used to practice savoring, children relate well to food items such as dried fruit, chocolate or candy, to be eaten slowly and meditatively. Here are the instructions for "savoring," using a piece of fresh or dried fruit (apple, raisin, orange, banana, date, fig, etc.).

Savoring Instructions

This 5-10 minute mindfulness exercise can be practiced in an office setting or recommended for home practice using a piece of fresh or dry fruit.

Begin by looking at the food item to observe its color, shape, texture and other physical qualities. Smell it to experience its odor. Is it fragrant and pleasing? Reflect on how it came to you now. From where did it come. . .a tree? Do you know where it grew? What helped it grow. . .sun, water and earth? How did it get from there to here? Take some time to appreciate all that was involved in bringing this food item to you, as well as the nourishment it will provide. Think of it as a concentrated form of energy that will be released when you ingest it, and what you might do with that energy.

Slowly take a bite, savoring its flavor and texture in your mouth. Notice the sensations as your tongue presses the food item against your teeth. Is there a burst of flavor? Take your time to experience the process of eating and nourishing your body with the food's latent energy. Notice if you are in a rush to take another bite, and see what happens when you do this. Compare that to chewing slowly, deliberately and mindfully.

You can practice this exercise with virtually any food item, including chocolate or candy. In such cases, you should modify the instructions to "slowly dissolving without biting into the food item" instead of "chewing slowly."

You can also apply this form of full attentiveness to other daily activities, such as brushing teeth attentively for at least two minutes (as dentists advise) or enjoying a warm bath.

Meditation for Preschool Children

Mental health professionals are now teaching and encouraging meditation practice with children and youth. Schools in some communities are also integrating mindfulness meditation practices as a way of readying children for learning. Even preschool children can learn and benefit from meditation using props and instructions designed for this age group.

One excellent resource for preschoolers is Lisa Desmond's book, *Baby Buddhas: A Guide to Teaching Meditation to Children* (2004), in which she addresses 2-3-year-old children. Desmond uses specific meditations, each of which addresses an emotional or behavioral issue. Some of the meditations are used to reduce anxiety. Below are some examples:

- **OM Meditation:**

    Uses: separation anxiety, when child feels anxious or afraid, or when a child needs comforting and reassurance. Also used to teach children to comfort themselves.

    Materials: soft pillow, folded blanket, or rug used indoors or outdoors.

    Instructions: have child place his or her hands over the heart and explain, "Your parents' love is always in your heart even when they are not with you. All the people who love you are right here in your heart. Whenever you need to feel that love, put your hands over your heart, rock gently and chant (sing), "Ommm, ommm, ommm. I love my home, I love my Mom, I love my Dad. Ommm, ommm, ommm." (Note that "Om" is the same sound as "om" in "home").

- **Cleansing Breath Meditation:**

    Uses: when a child needs to be calmed, to rid a child of fearful thought or feelings, to help a child face a new or anxiety-arousing situation, to help a child relieve stress or when a child needs to focus or calm down.

    Materials: soft meditation pillow, folded blanket, or rug used indoors or outdoors; singing bowl with striker, single-tone chime or bell.

    Instructions: "I am going to ring the bell (or strike the singing bowl). Listen until the sound ends and then we are going to breathe in slowly and deeply 3 times." As the child breathes in and out slowly, say, "Breathe in love and breathe out fear," or "Breathe in joy and breathe out anger," or "Breathe in peace and breathe out badness." Choose language that addresses the particular child's issues. You can begin this meditation by demonstrating a slow, deep breathing pattern. Children have a natural tendency to imitate.

- **Sunshine Meditation:**

    Uses: when a child needs to feel comfortable in a new or anxiety-arousing situation, right before any transition such as before going to school (or in a car on the way to visit friends or family).

    Materials: soft meditation pillow, folded blanket, or rug, or any place indoors or outdoors.

    Instructions: "We are going to sit with our legs crossed, our backs straight and our heads held up high. Our hands are crossed and placed over our hearts. Beneath your crossed hands is a ball of sunshine light, which is full of love. Every time you breathe in, your ball of sunshine lights gets bigger. Now we are going to fill ourselves up with this bright ball of sunshine light." Demonstrate long and slow breathing in and out, and say, "Bigger." Repeat 3 or 4 times and say, "Can you feel yourself all filled up with bright sunshine light and love?"

Martial Arts

Martial arts are generally viewed as self-defense skills, and this is an accurate understanding of their history and purpose. But martial arts are also self-regulation skills that have psychological benefits, such as self-confidence, mind-body connection, focus, discipline and self-empowerment. In addition, as an active self-regulation practice martial arts involve physical movement, and this is important for those anxious children who have difficulty sitting still and controlling impulses.

Martial arts are appropriate for children who are anxious and fearful. These skills and their emotional benefits are especially appropriate for victims of abuse or children with trauma histories. Martial arts also counteract feelings of vulnerability by empowering practitioners to "stand up to" challenges, not just by other people but also by life itself.

Here is an example from a socially anxious adolescent girl who was asked by her therapist to write about what helps her with anxiety.

How Aikido Changed My Life

Aikido has changed my life and I would not be the same person today without it in my life. During my junior high school and high school years I had an anxiety disorder. I always felt like an outsider and my self-esteem was low as a result. I felt nervous socially and whenever I would talk with someone I would not know what to say. I was afraid I would come off awkward at best or at the worst sound stupid to them. This fear of social rejection made me keep to myself because I thought people would not understand what it was like to have that fear. My stomach would also hurt and I would break out into sweat whenever I would talk to my peers. I never got comfortable in my own skin until I joined Aikido.

I was drawn to Aikido because it promotes peaceful conflict resolution and integrates relaxation into the techniques. I was really nervous when I first started Aikido but now that I look back almost two years later I'm glad I took a chance and joined Aikido. I learned interesting holds and empty hand techniques there as well as how to use a sword. But I really learned some deeper lessons from my Aikido practice. I learned not only new techniques but also how to handle new situations thrown at me suddenly to activate my anxiety disorder. I also stopped striving to be perfect and settled for the best I could do. I learned to reach out to people instead of isolating myself. I also learned that worry hinders you and holds you back. It becomes a vicious cycle: if you worry a lot all the things that you could be enjoying about life pass you by. My Aikido practice reinforced to me that you should just try to be yourself and be open to growing as a person. As a result, I learned my greatest lesson in Aikido. . .the lesson of self-acceptance and I found peace within myself.

Unless you are a martial arts instructor, the most ethical way to integrate this skill into therapy is to recommend martial art schools or academies that offer children's programs. Think of martial arts as an adjunctive self-regulation practice that can support and reinforce your therapy efforts.

Flow Activities

The mind-body state known as "flow" is similar to the Magic Word technique (relaxation response) and this is another way for children to counteract anxiety. Flow is a state in which we are engaged in activities to the extent that we lose track of time as well as of our sense of self as separate from the present activity (Csikszentmihalyi, 1990). In other words, in the flow state we become fully engaged and at one with an activity. It is virtually impossible to experience anxiety at the same time as flow because concentration and full engagement are required

Flow as an anti-anxiety state is accessible through a wide range of activities.

- Art (drawing, sketching, painting, sculpting, making collages)
- Crafts (needlepoint, knitting, crochet)
- Playing a musical instrument
- Listening to music
- Sports
- Exercise
- Yoga
- Meditation
- Relaxation practice
- Reading
- Journaling

However, there is one condition that must be met in order to experience the state of flow: there must be an optimal match between skill and challenge. That is, a child must have enough skill or proficiency in an activity so that it can be performed with ease or grace. Low skill and high challenge will result in frustration. For example, a child who has difficulty reading will experience frustration rather than flow with reading.

Some child clients have tried to convince me that playing video games puts them in flow. In fact, a recent research study found that children who played less than one hour of video games per day did *better* on some positive measures than children who played no video games at all (Przybylski, 2014). It appears that video gaming in moderation can be a healthy flow activity, so long as it is does not interfere with social life and behavioral health (sleep, eating, exercise). When activities compromise social life and health, they become addictive behaviors that need to be addressed.

You can incorporate flow into your work with anxious children with the following steps:

1. Define flow
2. Help identify each child's flow activities
3. Encourage new flow activities if child has none
4. Suggest scheduling time for flow activities
5. Follow up with journal log of flow time

Interventions For Anxiety Disorders

The *DSM-5*® Anxiety Disorders

The American Psychiatric Association (APA) published the *Diagnostic and Statistical Manual of Mental Disorders-4th Edition* (*DSM-IV*) in 1994. In that edition, the APA recognized that children experience all of the anxiety disorders observed in adults. Therefore, the *DSM-IV* combined the criteria for adult and child anxiety disorders, with just one exception. The diagnosis, Separation Anxiety, could not be used with adults. However, in the 5th edition, published in 2013, that exception was eliminated in recognition of the fact that adults can also experience separation anxiety. As a result, we now recognize just one set of anxiety disorders that applies to children, adolescents and adults.

Co-Occurring Disorders

A diagnostic system is an effort to categorize symptom patterns, but our clients do not always fit neatly into the diagnostic "boxes." Some children exhibit symptoms of more than one disorder, such as anxiety as well as attention deficits, hyperactivity, depression, bipolar disorder or autism spectrum behaviors. Sometimes the "co-occurring disorder" is actually a manifestation of anxiety. For example, we know that worry, the hallmark feature of generalized anxiety disorder, affects concentration and attention, which may be misdiagnosed as an attention-deficit disorder. Frequent worry also tends to interfere with sleep, which causes fatigue and exhaustion, symptoms that may be seen as depression.

Furthermore, anxiety sometimes manifests in the form of behavior problems. Since behavior can be considered a form of communication, anxiety may be "acted out" as temper tantrums, school refusal, or oppositional-defiant behavior when a child is attempting to avoid situations that may be anxiety-arousing. When you are dealing with a child referred due to a behavior problem, you are advised to consider the following question: "If the behavior had language, what would it say?" In other words, what feelings are being communicated behaviorally?

To sort out these diagnostic nuances, it may be helpful to include some anxiety screening tools. See Chapter 2 for a discussion and list of child anxiety screening tests that can be used to sort out the diagnostic overlap between anxiety and other conditions, such as attention deficit/hyperactivity disorder, oppositional defiant disorder and depression.

In most cases, however, a diagnosis of anxiety can be made without screening tools or psychological testing. A basic requirement is familiarity with the diagnostic criteria for the *DSM-5* disorders and a thorough initial interview procedure as discussed in Chapter 1. The rest of this chapter is focused on each of the anxiety conditions and the treatment approaches, strategies and interventions that are believed to be most effective.

Separation Anxiety Disorder (SAD)

It is considered common for children up to the age of 6 to experience anxiety or fear in relation to separation from their security figures, typically their parents or guardians. This is apparent when viewing the following chart of common fears in children and adolescents displayed by age range:

Common Fears in Children and Adolescents*

Age	Common Fears
0-6 months	Loss of support, loud noises
7-12 months	Strangers, sudden movements or large/looming objects
1 year	**Separation**, toilet, strangers
2 years	**Separation**, dark, animals, loud noises, large objects, changes in house
3-4 years	**Separation**, masks, dark, animals, noises at night
5 years	**Separation**, animals, "bad people," bodily harm
6 years	**Separation**, thunder and lightning, supernatural beings, dark, sleeping or staying alone, bodily injury
7-8 years	Supernatural beings, dark, fears based on television viewing, staying alone, bodily injury
9-12 years	Tests, school performance, physical appearance, thunder and lightning, bodily injury, death
14-15 years	Family and home issues, political concerns, preparation for future, personal appearance, social relations, school

*From Dr. Foxman's book, *The Worried Child* (pages 22-23)

The diagnosis of separation anxiety disorder may still be used for preschoolers when the severity of such anxiety is outside the normal range. This is a judgment call but it is usually not difficult to discern the difference between normal and abnormal separation anxiety. The following three symptom variables can be used to distinguish between normal and abnormal separation anxiety:

1. *Frequency*: how often does it occur?
2. *Intensity*: how severe when it occurs?
3. *Duration*: how long does it last

You can use these evaluative terms for all of the anxiety disorders to distinguish between symptoms that are within the normal range and those that cross the line to become a disorder that affects the ability to function in daily life.

Here are some empirically-based tools that can help differentiate between normal and abnormal separation anxiety, with source information in Silverman and Ollendick (2005).

- **Observation:** it is important to observe or obtain reliable reports of the child in multiple contexts, on numerous occasions, and in their everyday environments (home, daycare, preschool, school). It is also beneficial to view parent and child interactions and behaviors that may contribute to SAD. The Dyadic Parent-Child Interaction Coding System and recently the Dyadic Parent-Child Interaction Coding System II (DPICS II) are methods that can be used when observing parent and child interactions.

- **Self-report Measures:** child self-report should not be the sole basis of a SAD diagnosis, since children may not always have the cognitive and communication skills to give valid information about their experience. Nevertheless, input from children is important to understand their subjective experience. An example of a self-report tool that has been tested is the Separation Anxiety Assessment Scale for Children (SAAS-C). The scale contains 34 items and is divided into six dimensions. The dimensions in order are: abandonment, fear of being alone, fear of physical illness, worry about calamitous events, frequency of calamitous events, and safety signal index. The scale goes beyond assessing symptoms by focusing also on individual treatment planning.

- **Diaries and Behavior Logs:** separation anxiety daily diaries (SADD) can be used to assess anxious behaviors along with their antecedents and consequences. This assessment tool may be particularly suited to SAD given its specific focus on parent–child separation.

Criteria for Diagnosis of Separation Anxiety Disorder

At least 3 of the following criteria must be met to diagnose separation anxiety:

- Recurrent excessive distress when anticipating or experiencing separation from home or from major attachment figures

- Persistent and excessive worry about losing major attachment figures or about possible harm to them, such as illness, injury, disasters, or death

- Persistent and excessive worry about experiencing an adverse event (e.g., getting lost, being kidnapped, having an accident, becoming ill) that causes separation from a major attachment figure

- Persistent reluctance or refusal to go out, away from home, to school, to work, or elsewhere because of fear of separation

- Persistent and excessive fear of or reluctance about being alone or without major attachment figures at home or in other settings

- Persistent reluctance or refusal to sleep away from home or to go to sleep without being near a major attachment figure

- Repeated nightmares involving the theme of separation

- Repeated complaints of physical symptoms (e.g., headaches, stomachaches, nausea, vomiting) when separation from major attachment figures occurs or is anticipated

Once a diagnosis of separation anxiety disorder is made, attention can turn to therapy. Treatment for separation anxiety can take some important cues from the natural, gradual process by which a growing child normally learns to separate successfully from his or her security base. Children separate *gradually* from their security figures and learn to trust that the security base is constant and trustworthy. Piaget (1952), a developmental psychologist, used the French word *rapprochement* to describe this normal separation process. *Rapprochement,* from the Latin word, "approach," refers to the process of leaving and returning: a toddler crawls away from the security figure and then "re-approaches" to make contact with the security base to be assured of its "object constancy." The process builds gradually on itself in the direction of independence and autonomy.

In therapy, we need to establish a more formalized process that has several names, all of which refer to the use of exposure:

- Exposure therapy
- Systematic desensitization
- Graduated exposure
- Progressive exposure

All of these terms refer to a step-by-step process in which a client gradually faces an anxiety-arousing situation. Typically, the client first learns how to relax using one of the techniques described in Chapter 3. A series of steps are then taken in which the client spends an increasing amount of time "exposed" to the anxiety-arousing situation. In therapy, the pace of this process is negotiated between the therapist and client, and such collaboration is recommended even with children.

Take the following steps to use an exposure process with a child client to address separation anxiety.

1. **Explain the process:** "*We will work together to help you feel comfortable doing things in new situations without your parent(s) being present. We will decide on a series of steps you can take to get to the goal of feeling safe and relaxed.*"
2. **Introduce a 10-point scale:** "*Let's imagine a thermometer with marks on it ranging from 0 to 10. The 0 mark represents feeling safe and relaxed, and the 10 mark represents very high fear or anxiety. We can call it the 'fear thermometer', and you can use it as a way of expressing how you comfortable you feel.*"
3. **Teach a relaxation skill:** "*I will teach you a relaxation skill that will help you learn to feel safe and comfortable in new situations. If you practice your skill regularly, you will be more successful in facing difficult situations.*"
4. **Initiate progressive exposure with relaxation:** "*When you are ready, I will suggest that you spend a few minutes in new situations and use your relaxation skill to feel safe and comfortable. You can use the "fear thermometer" to express your anxiety level and see your progress. Using your relaxation skill in the new situation will help you make progress.*"
5. **Measure progress in terms of decreasing anxiety during exposure:** "*If you can lower your fear number in the new situation, even a little, you will be making progress and feel good about yourself. You can build on your brave steps by extending the amount of time you stay in the new situation.*"

Progress is measured in terms of decreasing anxiety during exposure, and the goal is "satiation" (low or no anxiety during exposure).

You can engage your child clients by collaborating on the *pace* of an exposure process. If you have invested in establishing trust and positive rapport, your child clients are more likely to take "risks" in facing feared situations such as separation. Remember that children's natural instinct is to avoid anxiety-arousing situations. Therefore, if you leave it completely up to the child to determine the pace of exposure it will take a long time. On the other hand, if you move too quickly the child may be overwhelmed by anxiety and experience setbacks as well as feel demoralized.

In many cases, it is the parents' difficulty letting go of their children that drives their children's separation anxiety. In other words, some parents have separation anxiety in relation to their children. You may observe this dynamic in the following parenting behaviors:

- Prolonged good-byes in waiting rooms or at school
- Lingering too long when it is appropriate to leave
- Speaking for the child
- Eavesdropping on your sessions with the child
- Frequent email communication from parents about the child's needs
- Distrust of professionals (therapists, teachers, school administrators)
- Taking the child to the classroom rather than separating outside the building

These parent behavior patterns do not necessarily indicate an issue with parent separation anxiety but they are clues to be investigated and addressed if necessary. It is recommended that you address these parenting behaviors with a sensitive remark, such as, *"I can see how much you love and care for your child. And yet I sense that you are struggling with the difficult process of letting go, and of trusting that your child will be in good hands."*

"Letting go" is an ongoing parenting challenge. The first letting-go experience is birthing, followed by what may seem like an endless series of letting-go moments, such as putting children in daycare, using a baby-sitter, sending children to summer camp, having them drive a car, going to college, etc. This is naturally challenging for parents who love their children and in whom the protective instinct is strong. However, parents can go too far in protecting and this can become a dysfunctional parenting style. These following terms have been used to describe the various manifestations of parental overprotectiveness.

- Helicopter parenting
- Bulldozer parenting
- Snowplow parenting

Empathy is the first step in helping parents who are struggling with letting go. You can express empathy by using self-disclosure, if appropriate in your case, by saying, *"As a parent, I understand how much trust it takes to step back and let your children deal with challenges, disappointments and frustrations. And yet this is necessary for them to learn the skills they will need to be successful in life."* With some parents, you might want to recommend that they seek support for the "letting-go" process by meeting with a therapist or parent counselor.

There are also some suggested readings that could be helpful. For example, in her book, *The Gift of Failure: How the Best Parents Learn to Let Go So Their Children Can Succeed* (2015), Lahey explains that early failure and its consequences help children develop a toolbox of skills to gain autonomy and competence for later in life. Similarly, in his book, *How Children Succeed: Grit, Curiosity and the Hidden Power of Character* (2012), Tough outlines the skills and character traits children attain by encountering and overcoming failure. Yet another perspective is offered in, *Necessary Losses* (1998), in which Voirst argues persuasively that through loss, including loss of our mothers' protection, we gain deeper perspective, true maturity, and fuller wisdom about life.

After you express empathy (using self-disclosure if appropriate in your case), parents struggling with letting go can be helped with an intervention, "Three Questions for Parent Separation Anxiety." Here are the three questions to help parents who are struggling with letting go:

Three Questions For Parent Separation Anxiety

1. As a parent, what are your goals for your children?
2. To achieve these goals, what skills will your children need and how will they attain those skills?
3. When should you start the process?

Most parents answer the first question with variations of, "for my children to be *independent*." Variations of this theme include, "successful," "resilient," "happy," and "make good decisions."

The purpose of the second question is to help parents see that to be independent their children need to have certain experiences, such as making decisions on their own, learning how to bounce back from failure or disappointment, and experiencing the natural consequences of bad decisions. This question is designed to help parents see the importance of stepping back and tolerating their children's adverse experiences because that is the foundation for new skills and autonomy. Parents need to learn how to be "guides" and "consultants" and resist the temptation to overprotect and do too much for their children.

The third question closes the loop by pointing out that the struggle to let go in the present is directly related to parent success in the future. Parents need to step back now in order to be successful in raising "independent," "successful," "resilient," "happy" adults who "make good decisions."

The "Three Questions Intervention" is appropriate for anxious parents who are overprotective and ambivalent about letting go. It is not appropriate for parents on the other end of the continuum—parents who are detached, depressed, uninvolved, narcissistic, or otherwise not engaged with their children. Those parents need support for becoming more "tuned in" and connected with their children.

Another intervention for anxious, overprotective parents is to bring their attention to the brief chapter, "On Children," from the classic book, *The Prophet* (Gibran, 1923). This book was originally published almost a century ago, has sold millions of copies and has been translated into over 20 languages. The book is spiritual in its wisdom but it is not religious, and the chapter on children seems to have a powerful impact on parents. I have read the two-page chapter, "On Children," to many parents and in some cases I have shown a YouTube video of the text accompanied by a touching photo essay (youtube.com/watch?v=ByPOnZqICfs).

The poignant message of the Gibran's chapter is that children come *through* but not *from* their parents, and that each child has a unique destiny to fulfill. The take-home message for parents is that their job is to love and care for their children but also to step back, let go and encourage them to discover their purpose in life.

You may also share a quote from Erich Fromm that addresses the parent letting-go issue in child separation anxiety. Speaking of motherly love but relevant to fathers who are connected to their children, Fromm (1978) asserts:

> The very essence of motherly love is to care for the child's growth, and that means to want the child's separation from herself. Here lies the basic difference to erotic love. In erotic love, two people who were separate become one. In motherly love, two people who were one become separate. The mother must not only tolerate, she must wish and support the child's separation. It is only at this stage that motherly love becomes such a difficult task, that it requires unselfishness, the ability to give everything and to want nothing but the happiness of the loved one (p. 232.)

Generalized Anxiety Disorder (GAD)

Generalized anxiety is the form of anxiety involving frequent and chronic worry. What is a worry?

The *DSM-5* defines a worry as *apprehensive expectation about one of more things (such as school, health or work) occurring more days than not for six months or more*. Worries are typically recognized as *excessive* and *unreasonable*, but the worrier is unable to control the worry pattern. Although there are "normal" worries of childhood and adolescence, worrying that interferes with the ability to function in daily life (impairment in attention, concentration, memory) crosses the line and becomes an anxiety disorder. In children, the areas most affected by generalized anxiety are social and academic. In addition, generalized anxiety also involves physical symptoms, including:

- Restlessness
- Feeling keyed up or on edge
- Fatigue
- Muscle tension
- Sleep disturbance

Research with children and adolescents finds developmentally "normal" worries. In the order of their frequency and intensity, the normal worries of both children and adolescents are:

1. School performance
2. Physical appearance (body image)
3. Social acceptance
4. Something bad happening to a parent
5. Something bad happening to a friend
6. Global worries (terrorism, war, climate change)

Normal worries are transient and do not cause significant impairment in ability to function in daily life. In contrast, here is an example of excessive and unreasonable worry in a ten-year-old boy referred for therapy: "I worry about death because it is forever. And I worry about not getting married and getting a good job." This boy's worries were developmentally out of sync with his age and they were causing significant subjective distress. In addition, their negative effect on attention and concentration this boy's worries were impairing his school performance.

Worry can be thought of as an attempt to feel in control in the face of uncertainty and ambiguity. We worry to acquire a sense of control by anticipating what might happen and trying to prepare in advance. This does not work well because we cannot predict the future. Worrying results in a state of anxious arousal and typically results in subjective distress. In addition, since worries are invariably negative there is a high correlation between worry and depression.

Effective treatment for generalized anxiety involves identifying worry as a habit, and practicing alternative thought patterns. It can be helpful to spend some time exploring the positive alternatives to worry by asking questions, such as, *"What will you have more of if you were to worry less?"* or *"With what new ways of thinking and behaving will you replace worry?"* Young clients will usually recognize the following positive goals:

- Sleep better
- Have more energy
- Be more relaxed
- Think positively
- More confidence in ability to handle future problems
- More enjoyment in present activities

There are many strategies that can move child and adolescent clients towards the goals listed above. They include the following interventions, each of which will be described in detail:

Reframing "Harmless" Worries

Worries can be classified into two groups:

> "Harmless:" Harmless worries are about things that would do no significant harm if they were to happen. An example of a harmless worry is: "What if the school bus is late?"

> "Tragic." Tragic worries are about things that would have a significant or devastating effect if they were to happen. An example of a tragic worry is: "What if the school bus runs off the road in a storm and we crash and die?"

With this distinction in mind, have your child or adolescent client write down his or her worries on a sheet of paper. For the harmless worries, suggest that the client add the word, *"So. . ."* to the beginning of each harmless worry statement. For the harmless worry example above, the statement would read, *"So what if the bus is late?"* The goal of this intervention is to demonstrate that the time and energy in such worrying is out of proportion to the worry and, therefore unproductive and unnecessary.

Reality-testing "Tragic" Worries

Reality-testing is a process of evaluating the reasonableness of our own thinking. For worry, the goal is to recognize the *improbability* of the tragic worry happening, even though it could be devastating if it were to actually happen. For example, a school bus running off the road with children aboard could be tragic but it is highly unlikely to happen. You can reassure the worried child that bus drivers have special commercial driver's licenses as well as the skill and experience to drive buses safely.

Externalizing Worries

Externalizing a worry means finding ways to put a worry thought in a physical form, such as writing on paper and placing it in a "worry jar" or "worry box." While this a symbolic gesture or metaphor with adults, with children, who are more concrete, this can serve to temporarily relieve the mind of worry thoughts. Here are several suggestions for externalizing a child's worries:

- Have the child write his or her worries on paper, one piece of paper for each worry. Suggest a place to keep the worries, such as a jar or box. A further step would be to suggest that the child only think about the worry if it is taken out of the jar or box. Making a worry container in the therapy office can be a craft project. There are also commercially available worry-boxes that look like small mailboxes with slots into which a child can put written and folded worries.

- For young children (up to age 9 or 10 depending on maturity level), suggest that the parents purchase a set of Guatemalan worry dolls (available online or from folk art stores). The child is instructed to give one worry to each doll before going to bed at night, and put the dolls under their pillow. The accompanying instruction sheet states that according to legend, when children wake up the following morning their worries are gone! While this may not actually be true, the power of suggestion can render the Guatemalan worry dolls helpful in reducing insomnia in generalized anxiety disorder. I keep a few sets of Guatemalan worry dolls on hand in my office and sometimes I will gift a set to a child with whom I am working. This can help with continuity of therapy from office to home.

- With older children and adolescents, you can suggest that the written worries be kept close at hand, such as in a pocket or wallet. The instructions in this case are to feel free to think about the worries but only if the specific written worry is opened up and in hand. This intervention is based on the idea that one step in controlling worry is to take charge of *when* a young person decides to think about a worry. In effect, this intervention encourages the young person to decide when to spend time thinking about his or her worries.

Prescribing the Symptom

This paradoxical intervention is based on the theory of *exposure*. The idea is that by purposefully focusing on worries, they will lose their power and diminish in intensity.

Suggest that the child or adolescent choose a "worry time" once each day. The length of the worry time is left up to the child but advise that it should not be just before bedtime. You can guide the young client as to an appropriate worry time: 5 minutes for young children and up to 20 minutes for adolescents. The instructions are to focus on the current worries or troublesome thoughts for the entire worry time.

However, if the worry thoughts come to mind at any other time the child is advised to think, *"Not now, come back at worry time."*

Positive Affirmations

Worries are always negative. Rarely do people worry about positive events except when something negative is associated with a positive occurrence, such having to make an acceptance speech for a high achievement award or being faced with increased responsibilities as a result of a job promotion. Therefore, one strategy for counteracting worry is to create a positive affirmation for clients with chronic worry.

A positive affirmation should be thoughtfully crafted to counteract a client's key worry or negative thought. Collaborating with the child client, build a concise statement that affirms the opposite of the client's core worry. The client is advised to repeat the positive affirmation several times each time he or she thinks a worry thought. Four criteria should be considered when creating a positive affirmation. Here are the instructions:

Instructions for Positive Affirmations

Create a positive statement that counteracts a worry thought and that meets these four criteria:

1. Present tense
2. Action verb
3. Self-referenced
4. Realistically positive

Sample affirmations (ask client to guess the underlying worry in each case):

- "I accept mistakes as necessary for learning."
- "My parents love me and can be trusted to take good care of me."
- "I trust my ability to do well in school."
- "I exercise regularly and live a healthy life."
- "I enjoy the here and now."
- "I do my best in school and have grades that reflect my efforts."

Mindfulness

Mindfulness, defined as: "awareness of present experience without judgment," can be an effective practice for reducing worry. As applied to worry, mindfulness helps clients view worry objectively as a habit that does not need to be taken personally or identified as "mine." This could be called "Witnessing" and these are the instructions:

Witnessing Instructions

Notice and label your thoughts without judgment and say one of these witnessing self-statements to yourself:

- "That's just my worry habit."
- "A thought is not a fact."
- "It's not happening now."
- "What are my behavior choices?"
- "Don't believe everything you think."

Miracle Question

The Miracle Question, published by Steve de Shazer (1988), is an intervention to enhance solution focused therapy. The theory underlying this approach is that clients are more likely to be successful in achieving their goals if they can describe what life would be like if the problem that brought them to therapy has been resolved. The Miracle Question is an intervention that directs your clients' attention to their desired outcomes and how they will know they have been successful. The Miracle Question can be asked at any time during the course of therapy. Here is a version that can be used with children and adolescents:

> "When you leave my office today, imagine that a miracle occurs. As a result of the miracle you no longer have the worry problem we have been discussing. However, the miracle occurs tonight while you are sleeping so you won't know that it has happened until you wake up tomorrow morning. What will be different, what will you notice and how will you know that you have changed?"

Letter from the Future

The Letter from the Future is an assignment that can be suggested for adolescent clients with the worry form of anxiety. It is designed to counteract the negative story that worriers tell themselves about the future. Similar to the Miracle Question, the Letter from the Future is designed to bring your client's attention to what it would be like to overcome the worry habit. Your client is asked to imagine a future without the worry habit and write a letter from that perspective to the current self. Here are the instructions:

> "Imagine that you are at a future point in time, when you are older and no longer have the anxiety we have been discussing. Write a letter from your future self to your current self, describing what you are doing, what it's like and what steps you took to get there. Include what you learned that helped you get there. End with some wise advice to yourself."

Playing the Part

This intervention is based on the idea that we can practice acting *as if* we have resolved a specific problem, such as worrying. By "rehearsing" new behavior patterns, we can grow into the ability to function with less worry and anxiety. You can explain that this is exactly what good movie stars do and why they are successful in convincing us that they are the character they are pretending to be. You can ask your client to name one of their favorite movie stars and some of the movies in which they did a convincing job. You could also call this the "fake it until you make it" technique. Here are the instructions:

> "Imagine that you are auditioning for a part in a play. The character is a relaxed, confident and easy-going person who trusts that things will work out in the future. The character has a positive attitude and enjoys activities in the present. In addition, the character sleeps well and has high energy. To get the part you will need to be convincing. What behaviors, mannerisms, style of dress and other qualities will you need to be convincing. Let's try practicing right now."

Panic Disorder and Agoraphobia

Panic disorder is the form of anxiety involving panic attacks and their feared implications or consequences. A panic attack is a sudden and intense arousal response that is typically experienced as coming "out of the blue." A panic attack can include any of the following symptoms:

- Heart palpitations, pounding heart or accelerated heart rate
- Sweating
- Trembling or shaking
- Sensations of shortness of breath or smothering
- Feeling of choking
- Chest pain or discomfort
- Nausea or abdominal distress
- Feeling dizzy, unsteady, lightheaded or faint
- De-realization (feelings of unreality) or depersonalization (feelings of detachment)
- Fear of losing control or going crazy
- Fear of dying
- Numbness or tingling sensations
- Chills or hot flashes

It is appropriate to use the diagnosis of panic disorder *without* agoraphobia when a person experiences recurrent panic attacks and develops a persistent concern about having additional attacks, as well as worry about the consequences of the panic attacks, such as losing control, having a heart attack or dying. However, it is common for a pattern of behavioral avoidance to develop as a coping mechanism. This is the basis for a diagnosis of panic disorder *with* agoraphobia. In such cases, situations in which a person anticipates having panic attacks (because they are same or similar to the situation in which panic attacks have occurred before) are *avoided*. Avoidance is a coping style or defense mechanism, an instinctive way to manage panic anxiety. With young people, this may take the form of refusing to go to school and may result in becoming homebound. Another variation consists of avoiding situations in which there is a feeling of being trapped or confined, such as elevators, limited access highways, bridges, as well as movie theatres, churches and social situations where exiting would be inconvenient or draw attention. In other cases, such situations are *endured* with high anxiety or distress. Panic disorder with agoraphobia is the most common variation of this anxiety condition.

The success rate for treating panic disorder with agoraphobia is high, with reports up to 80% effectiveness with appropriate therapy. The phases of successful treatment can be broken down into the following steps:

1. **Diagnosis:** include a medical assessment to rule out any organic conditions that would account for the anxiety symptoms (e.g. hyperthyroidism, balance and inner ear syndromes, heart arrhythmias). Here are some of the medical conditions with symptoms may be mistaken for panic anxiety:

   - Hyperthyroidism
     – Nervousness, anxiety, irritability, heart racing, sleep issues, hand tremors
   - Balance & inner ear syndromes
     – Vertigo, dizziness, sweating, nausea
   - Heart arrhythmias
     – Palpitations, racing heart, dizziness, fainting, shortness of breath

2. **Reassurance:** naming the condition can in itself be reassuring. Reporting the high therapy success rate (80%) can further reassure your client and help with motivation. Adding information about your professional experience and success rate can also boost your credibility and offer reassurance.

3. **Relaxation:** begin as early as the second therapy visit to teach a relaxation skill and encourage daily practice.

4. **"Floating Technique":** build on relaxation with this intervention.

The Floating Technique was published by a pioneer in treating what was at the time called agoraphobia, now known as panic disorder with agoraphobia (Weekes, 1978). Although Weekes worked with adults, this technique is appropriate and effective with children and adolescents. There are four steps in this process:

- **Facing:** the concept is that progress and recovery requires facing, rather than avoiding, anxiety-arousing situations.
- **Accepting:** the concept is that panic anxiety can be experienced as a *practice opportunity*, a chance to use relaxation skills to handle a phobic situation in order to develop confidence.
- **Floating:** this key step involves relaxing through the sensations of anxiety as though one is floating or surfing on gently undulating water.
- **Let time pass:** this step involves reminding oneself that every panic anxiety experience will pass in a few minutes. There may be a stream of panic "attacks" but each will be short lived and pass.

With adults you can use the analogy of childbirth preparation classes to make the point that floating involves breathing through the anxiety sensations, which is an unnatural and counter-intuitive response to pain. In childbirth preparation classes, expectant mothers are encouraged to resist the instinct to tense up and hold the breath. The idea is to practice doing the opposite: breathe through the experience.

With children, it would make more sense to use other analogies, such as asking, *"How come trees don't break when the wind blows?"* The idea is to *be flexible* or *bend with* the anxiety and let it blow through like wind through the trees.

It is also important to stress that *practice* is necessary to overcome this disorder. You can use a sports analogy, such as practicing basketball foul shots in advance so that when it really counts the player will have a better chance of being successful.

The goal of the Floating Technique is to develop confidence that with the requisite relaxation skill your young client can move more gracefully through panic anxiety and do so with less fear. As confidence develops, the probability of panic anxiety diminishes and, when it does occur, the frequency, intensity and duration of anxiety tend to decrease.

Obsessive-Compulsive Disorders (OCD, Trichotillomania And Excoriation)

There are two key words in the name of this anxiety disorder: obsessions and compulsions. What is the relationship between the two components?

- **OBSESSIONS** are persistent and unwanted thoughts, images or urges accompanied by negative feelings (anxiety, guilt, disgust, shame). Because they are unwanted, obsessions cause additional anxiety or distress and the person usually attempts to ignore or suppress them by replacing them with other thoughts or ritualized actions. Obsessions typically fit one of these categories:

    - Contamination

    - Aggressive impulses or urges

    - Sexual preoccupations or urges

    - Magical/superstitious

    - Somatic issues

- **COMPULSIONS** are the time-consuming, ritualized behaviors designed to reduce the negative feelings associated with obsessions. Compulsions are not connected in a realistic way with the negative thoughts, urges or feelings that they are designed to reduce. They include the following behavior patterns:

    - Cleaning/washing

    - Checking

    - Ordering/arranging/symmetry

    - Counting

    - Repeating

    - Hoarding/collecting

PANDAS

A form of OCD, known as PANDAS (pediatric autoimmune neuropsychiatric disorders associated with streptococcal infections), has recently been recognized. This is a controversial diagnosis that refers to sudden onset OCD symptoms often accompanied by neuromuscular tics in children who test positive for streptococcus bacteria (but who may have not have "strep throat" or other bacterial infection symptoms). These are the conditions under which this diagnosis might be used:

- Abrupt, episodic OCD symptoms and/or tic disorder
- Average age of onset: 6.3 years
- 2.6 times more likely in boys
- Associated with history of strep infection
- Frequently associated with ADHD-like symptoms

The treatment for PANDAS is a medical intervention, typically prolonged antibiotic medication up to 30 days. In some cases, blood transfusions have been used to clear up the bacterial infection. Psychotherapy may still be appropriate to address anxiety and support a child through the medical procedures. If you are dealing with a child exhibiting sudden OCD symptoms and you use a development history form, such as the one in Chapter 1, you should look for a recent history of "strep throat" or other evidence of streptococcal infections to help make the diagnosis and refer for a medical evaluation. However, a child can test positive for the streptococcal bacteria without strep throat or other obvious symptoms. The key diagnostic step is to focus on the child's OCD history: were there early signs of OCD or did the condition seem to appear suddenly?

Treatment of Obsessive-Compulsive Disorder:

Since compulsions are defense mechanisms or coping strategies whose purpose is to relieve the uncomfortable feelings generated by obsessions, the most effective therapy strategy is to find an alternative source of relief. Building on relaxation training, the goal is to discover an alternative way to reduce tension and the uncomfortable feelings activated by obsessions.

When a substitute means of reducing tension and uncomfortable feelings does not seem to be effective, a more formal process, known as Exposure and Response Prevention (ERP), is indicated. This procedure also requires a foundation of relaxation practice. The theory behind ERP is that repeated and/or prolonged exposure to uncomfortable feelings will reduce anxious feelings and compulsive behaviors. Initially, however, exposure tends to *increase* anxiety.

ERP involves the following steps:

1. Explain the process
2. Teach relaxation skill
3. Establish stimulus hierarchy with anxiety baselines

4. Combine relaxation with "exposure" to the anxiety stimulus while "preventing" the compulsive "response"
5. Self-rate anxiety level at 2-3 minute intervals using a 10-point scale or "fear thermometer"
6. Measure progress as reduced anxiety during step 4

Let's apply the ERP protocol to a case of a child exhibiting a contamination obsession with frequent hand-washing rituals. Think of the hand washing as the "response" to feeling contaminated or dirty. Touching something that might be contaminated, such as doorknobs, handles or banisters, would be considered an "exposure" experience. Now, the treatment approach is to encourage the child to "prevent" hand washing as a response to the "exposure" of touching something he or she considers to be contaminated. Instead of hand washing, the child is encouraged to move through the anxious feelings using self-relaxation. Even a 10-15-minute delay in hand washing could be considered progress, and should be praised or rewarded. The goal is to reduce and ultimately eliminate compulsive behavior patterns by using more efficient, socially appropriate and effective ways to feel safe.

In some cases, a child with obsessive thinking may not yet have developed a compulsion response. In such cases, it is advisable to treat the obsessive cognitive style using the same strategies and intervention that were discussed earlier for worries (see Generalized Anxiety Disorder).

Trichotillomania (Hair-Pulling Disorder)

Hair pulling is a compulsive behavior pattern recognized in the *DSM-5* as an anxiety-based habit. Trichotillomania involves pulling hair from any part of the body resulting in bare spots. The most common areas of the body are the scalp, eyebrows and eyelids. Negative feelings, such as shame, embarrassment or feelings of loss of control, are common, and trichotillomania can impair social, occupational or school functioning due to avoidance of social interaction or absenteeism from work or school. Trichotillomania is not to be confused with twisting or playing with one's hair, or with hair removal for cosmetic purposes. Hair pulling is more common in females than males, with approximately 75% of cases being female.

The diagnostic criteria for trichotillomania consist of the following symptoms:

- Recurrent pulling of one's own hair, resulting in hair loss
- Repeated attempts to decrease or stop hair pulling
- The hair pulling causes significant distress or impairment in social, occupational, school or other important areas of functioning

It would be helpful to think of hair pulling as a compulsive behavior whose purpose is to reduce tension. Naturally, bare spots can be socially embarrassing, which is a high price to pay for the tension-reducing benefit. What drives this type of non-suicidal self-harm behavior?

From a treatment viewpoint, trichotillomania, a form of non-suicidal self-harm, can be considered an addictive behavior in that it produces a biochemical high that seems to make the negative consequences tolerable. Biochemistry drives trichotillomania (and excoriation); endorphins, narcotic-like chemicals produced in the brain are released in response to pain and this produces a mild euphoria.

One other consideration is that hair pulling is sometimes done without conscious awareness. Children, adolescents and adults with the hair pulling compulsion generally know they do this but they do not always know *when* they are doing it. See treatment strategies, below, for addressing this aspect of the hair pulling condition.

Treatment for Trichotillomania

As with treatment of addictions, trichotillomania can be addressed by discovering alternative, healthier ways to feel high or at ease. The feeling that results from compulsive hair pulling could be described as a combination of relaxation (tension release) and mild euphoria. What seems to be effective in achieving a similar feeling is an activity using the same fine motor muscles as in hair pulling, providing an alternative sensory activity that can compete with hair pulling for tension release. I use an organic beeswax product manufactured by Stockmar, available online and from some art supply stores. The product is a box of rectangular-shaped pieces of natural beeswax, available in two versions. The appropriate choice for use in therapy is the thicker, molding-wax version whereas the thinner version is used for candle decorating. The package of molding beeswax contains an assortment of colors, each of which has a characteristic natural aroma that adds to its soothing quality. At room temperature, the beeswax wafers are hard, like wood. However, when it is warmed up and worked in the hands for several minutes it becomes soft and pliable. Offer one piece to a child with the following instructions:

> **Stockmar Beeswax for Trichotillomania**
>
> *"Take a piece of beeswax from this box, in any color you want. Carry it with you at all times, and whenever you feel an urge to pull your hair, take out your beeswax and warm it up in your hands. Using the same fingers as when you pull your hair, squeeze and fold the beeswax over and over until it becomes soft and pliable. It will take a few minutes to do this. When it is soft, mold it into a shape such as a ball, a cube, a noodle or any shape you want. Then put it away until you need to use it again. It will get hard quickly as it cools, so next time you take it out you will have to warm it up again by squeezing and folding it over and over again.*
>
> *It will also help if you can choose someone in school, such as your teacher or a friend, and someone at home, such as a parent or sibling, who can let you know when you are starting to pull your hair. They can help alert you to the times when you are hair pulling without realizing it. They can be partners in your effort to get control over your hair pulling."*

Excoriation (Skin-Picking Disorder)

Skin-picking disorder shares many of the behavior patterns and nuances as hair-pulling disorder. Recently recognized as an anxiety-based pattern, skin picking is a compulsive condition involving recurrent picking at one's own skin. Typically the most commonly affected areas are the face, arms and hands, but many cases involve multiple body parts. Many individuals pick with their fingernails but in some cases tweezers, pins and other objects are used. Skin picking can be considered a tension-relieving compulsion and, like hair pulling, it results in a mild biochemically-based euphoric feeling.

The physical consequences of compulsive skin picking may include skin lesions and scars. Psychologically, the consequences may include feelings of embarrassment and shame about not being in control of the behavior. Compulsive skin picking may also impair social, occupational or school functioning in part due to social avoidance.

The diagnostic criteria for excoriation consist of the following symptoms:

- Recurrent skin picking resulting in skin lesions
- Numerous attempts to decrease or stop skin picking
- The skin picking causes significant distress in social, occupational, school or other important areas of functioning

Adolescent Self-Description of Excoriation

Here is a self-description of the condition written for her therapist by a 16-year-old girl. Note what she says sometimes helps as well as what does not help:

Important Times:

- 12 years old—first signs of it
- 14 years old—first heard the name for it
- About 18 months ago—realized I probably had it
- About 6 months ago—told my best friend
- About 1 month ago—told my boyfriend

What is it?

- Excoriation is a disorder that causes people to pick at their skin. They scratch, pick, pop, bite, etc. at things that my not even be there. It has no cure and while there are things you can do to manage it, it's just something I have to deal with. And probably always will.
- If I can't pick whatever it is then it starts to itch. It starts to hurt. I want to tear my skin off and get rid of it. I can't not touch it. And if I try to keep myself from picking then when I finally do it will be so much worse. I will not only pick that one thing. I will pick at twenty other things, too. And that's a low estimate.

How do I know I have it?

- I pick at my skin when there's nothing there. And I make something be there. I have scars on my shoulders and face because I have ripped my skin. I have had days where I have spent five hours picking my skin.

What helps?

- Fidget toys—sometimes they don't though
- Covering it

    If I can see it then I'm more likely to pick it

    While I am covering it I might pick it

    Once I'm triggered by seeing it I have to get it

What does not help?

- Telling me to stop
- Telling me it gets better
- Trying to compare it to you picking your skin
- Telling me I can stop
- Not letting me pick

Treatment for Excoriation

Skin picking can be addressed using the same strategies recommended above for hair pulling disorder. Children and youth should be asked to agree that trusted adults or friends can let them know when they are observed to be skin picking. This allows for in-the-moment implementation of alternative tension release strategies, such as the use of beeswax as described above for hair pulling. This strategy will not be effective for clients whose primary time for skin picking is when they are alone or in private. Nevertheless, the use of beeswax or a similar product is an effective strategy for substituting a soothing sensation using the same neuro-musculature involved in skin picking.

In some cases there may be some body dysmorphic dynamics that need to be addressed in therapy. When compulsive skin picking is associated with body dysmorphia, it is advisable to include a focus on the issues of perfectionism and self-esteem. For example, some clients may be hyper-focused on skin imperfections that they try to correct with skin picking. They may use magnifying mirrors to monitor pimples or blackheads, and take pleasure in squeezing their skin. Even though cosmetic skin picking is not considered a form of excoriation, excoriation may be embedded in body dysmorphic disorder, now classified in the obsessive-compulsive and related disorders category.

Social Anxiety Disorder

Social anxiety disorder, also referred to as social phobia, is a self-esteem-based anxiety condition in which a person projects onto others his or her own self view. Children and adolescents with social anxiety tend to have distorted views of themselves along with irrational concerns about their intelligence, appearance, social skills or other qualities. They fear that others will scrutinize or judge them negatively. Social anxiety can be intense especially for those who are shy or emotionally inhibited, and these traits are high risk factors for this anxiety disorder.

These are the criteria for a diagnosis of social anxiety disorder:

- An intense, irrational and persistent (lasting more than six months) fear of possible scrutiny or negative judgment by others.

- In children, the anxiety must occur in peer settings as well as during interaction with adults. Such anxiety can take the form of crying, tantrums, freezing, clinging, or failing to speak in social situations.

- Fear of acting in a way that will be embarrassing, humiliating, offensive or lead to rejection by others.

- Feared social or performance situations typically provoke an immediate anxious reaction ranging from diffuse apprehension to situational panic.

- The types of fears and avoidance commonly associated with social anxiety are to some degree experienced by most people, but in social anxiety the fear is out of proportion to actual danger or threat.

- To meet the diagnostic criteria for this disorder, the symptoms must be severe enough to cause significant distress or disability.

- Social anxiety can be generalized, meaning fear of many or most social interactions, or it can be limited to one situation, such as public speaking or performing.

Many situations can evoke social anxiety. Here are some of the common social phobic situations:

- Public speaking
- Interviews
- Playing music or singing to audience
- Athletic performance
- Speech and language (selective mutism)
- Dating (intimacy, sex)
- Public restrooms (paruresis)

Strategies for Social Anxiety

The strategies to be used to address social anxiety disorder focus on two primary areas: self-esteem and desensitization.

Self-Esteem Work:

Self-esteem is a key issue because a concern about being judged negatively or scrutinized by other people is often a projection onto others of how the socially anxious person views himself or herself. Young clients with low self-esteem are likely to be concerned that others will view them negatively, as unattractive, unintelligent, awkward or deficient in some way. In contrast, young clients with high self-esteem are more likely to assume that others will see them is a positive light.

Under normal circumstances, there are two sources of positive self-esteem. One is positive input from others, preferably primary caregivers early in life. Such input includes praise as well as healthy attachments to parents and other adults. Therapeutically, look for opportunities to give your client compliments and positive input. You can also suggest an assignment in which compliments are elicited from others. On the following pages are three letters that you can adapt or modify and give to your client or parents for this purpose:

Accepting Compliments: Parent

Dear Parent:

This is an important point in therapy for your child because she is working on self-esteem and self-confidence. High self-esteem is the basis of comfortable social communication as well as general happiness.

I would like to enlist your special help by asking that you give spontaneous compliments to your child as often as possible during the next week or two. Experts have found that the most useful way to give a compliment is to comment on specific aspects of a person's behavior. For example, "Holly, it's wonderful to see you getting to bed on time," or "Holly, we are proud of your willingness to take some risks in reaching out to your friends."

Your child is practicing accepting such positive feedback by making eye contact and saying, "Thank you."

I appreciate your help.

Sincerely,

_____

Accepting Compliments: Adult

Dear Reader:

The person handing you this letter is learning the skill of accepting a compliment. This is part of an overall lesson on self-esteem, which is the basis of comfortable social communication as well as general happiness.

We would like to enlist your special help by asking that you give spontaneous compliments as often as possible during the next week or two. Experts have found that the most useful way to give a compliment is to comment on specific aspects of a person's behavior or work that is positive, pleasing or courageous. For example, "Holly, you really impressed me with how you handled that challenge. It must have been difficult but you stepped up to it," or "Holly, I was impressed with how you took a risk and initiated contact with a friend."

The receiver of compliments is practicing accepting positive feedback by making eye contact and saying, "Thank you." We appreciate your help in giving this person several opportunities to practice this skill.

Sincerely,

_____

Accepting Compliments: Friend

Dear Friend:

The person giving you this note is learning the skill of accepting compliments. You can help by giving several compliments to your friend when your friend least expects it.

Experts have found that the most useful way to give a compliment is to comment on what a person does. For example, "You picked out a good sweater to go with those jeans. I like the way it looks," or "That pass you made in the second half was awesome. . .really good."

The receiver of compliments is practicing accepting positive feedback by making eye contact and saying, "Thank you." Your help in giving this person several opportunities to practice this skill is really appreciated.

Sincerely,

_____

The second source of self-esteem is the experience of success, competence and mastery that derives from solving problems and learning new skills. These experiences are empowering and activate good feelings and self-efficacy. Therefore, you can encourage your socially anxious child and adolescent clients to develop a new skill that, with practice, will help them feel successful and competent. The range of possible self-esteem building skills and activities is unlimited. As a starting point, you can explore areas of interest that can translate into skills and activities to pursue. Some possibilities are:

- Sports and fitness
- Learning to play a musical instrument
- Cooking
- Arts and crafts

Volunteer Position or Part-Time Job Involving Interaction with Others:

This is a variation of exposure therapy in which the socially anxious young person is encouraged to practice interacting with others in a defined role structure. This could consist of tutoring a younger child, volunteer work, or a part-time after school or weekend job in a store that involves interacting with customers. The goal is help the young client desensitize to social communication and interaction.

Group Therapy

Group therapy is one of the most powerful forms of treatment for social anxiety, but the idea of participating in a therapy group is likely to raise anxiety for clients with social phobia. Group work is effective because it is a form of exposure therapy that provides an opportunity to desensitize to social interaction. Group therapy will initially raise anxiety since it represents the very situation—social interaction—that is difficult for the shy or socially anxious person. Therefore, rather than making a commitment to participate in regular group therapy, it may help to encourage your socially anxious client to give this treatment modality a try by attending at least one group therapy session.

Despite the effectiveness of group therapy, it may be difficult to find group therapy opportunities in your community, particularly for children and adolescents. Therefore, you are encouraged to consider offering group therapy as one of your services for young people who are shy or suffering from social anxiety. As a bonus, if you are a therapist in private practice you will find that the income from group therapy exceeds the income from individual therapy for the same amount of time. Even a small group of four to six clients attending a 90-minute group therapy session will generate more income than an equivalent 90 minutes of individual therapy. In addition, agencies burdened by waiting lists or high demands for therapy services can use group therapy as one way to meet the need. Group therapy can be time-limited with a predetermined number of sessions or an open-ended group in which clients participate as long as the experience proves helpful.

Here are some steps to follow for offering a therapy group for social anxiety:

- Begin by creating a flier that describes the group you intend to start. Here is an example:

Social Anxiety Therapy Group

Lauren Mizus, M.A., MSW

Center for Anxiety Disorders

Location: 112 Lake Street, Burlington, Vermont

Telephone: (802) 865-3450

Time: Wednesdays from 5:30 p.m.

Description: This therapy and support group is designed for clients with social anxiety conditions, avoidant behavior, and shyness. We meet weekly to discuss strategies and skills for becoming more comfortable and confident in social interaction. The meetings begin with individual progress reports, followed by discussion of common themes and issues. While leading the meetings, Lauren will provide information and techniques known to be effective for social anxiety.

The group is open-ended. New members may join at any time and continue as long as the group is helpful. This allows new members to benefit from the positive experiences and progress of those who are farther down the road. "Older" members have an opportunity to review key information and skills, as well as to stabilize their progress.

Admissions Procedure: Clients interested in participating should call Lauren at 865-3450, Ext 403 to set up an initial interview. Health care professionals and others are welcome to call Lauren to discuss patient referrals. Health insurance is accepted.

- The first group therapy meeting is an opportunity to practice social communication in a structured exercise known as a "mutual interview." The group is organized into pairs of two partners. Everyone is given a sheet of paper with a list of questions to ask the person they are interviewing. The questions ask for the person's name, age, school name and grade, family members, favorite music, hobbies or interests, and what brought them to therapy. Each group member interviews his or her partner. The partners then reverse roles. After the pairs complete their interviews, a circle is formed and each member introduces the person they just interviewed to the whole group. A game can then be played in which anyone may direct a question to any other member, but the person who interviewed that member must guess the answer. For example, someone might ask a member of the group, "Do you have a pet at home?" The person who interviewed that member must guess the answer. This exercise is a warm-up activity for the first therapy group meeting and accomplishes the task of becoming acquainted in dyads (one-on-one interaction). This activity also tends to reduce anxiety as it becomes clear that everyone in the room has similar issues with social anxiety.

- There are many therapy activities that can be used in a therapy group for addressing social anxiety. The activities include learning relaxation skills (using any of the relaxation practices described in Chapter 3), role playing (e.g. how to start a conversation with someone you don't know), practicing eye contact (have partners look into each other's eyes without speaking and while using a relaxation skill), show-and-tell (e.g. each member plays a favorite song on an iPod and explains why it is a favorite song), and suggested assignments (e.g. self-esteem exercise described earlier in this chapter, return an item to a store for refund or credit, try a new skill and report back to the group).

- It is also important for many young clients to develop skill in assertive communication, and this skill can be taught and practiced in a group therapy setting. Assertiveness is typically anxiety-arousing, especially in situations with potential for conflict with other people. Dealing with bullying situations, questioning a teacher about a grade, asking parents for more independence, and setting limits in relationships are all examples of such situations. For such situations, you can teach the following 4-step formula for assertive communication (example for a student-teacher issue):

    1. empathy statement: "I know you are busy but there is something I need to talk about with you. Is this a good time?"
    2. express feeling or need using "I" statements: "I am disappointed in the grade I received on my essay and I would appreciate more feedback on what is missing."
    3. proposing a solution: "I would like to resubmit my essay with your input in mind."
    4. get agreement, "Would this be possible?"

- Group therapy offers a structured format for social interaction. With children and adolescents, it is also advisable to have a snack period, which creates an opportunity for spontaneous interaction. This offers an exposure experience for dealing with informal social situations.

Mentoring Programs

Mentoring is an increasingly popular way of providing guidance and support to young people. Recent years have seen youth mentoring expand from a relatively small youth intervention for children in need (usually for youth from single-parent homes) to a cornerstone youth service that is being implemented in schools, community centers, faith institutions, school-to-work programs, and a wide variety of other youth-serving institutions.

Mentoring programs consist of pairing an older or more experienced person with a client for the purposes of role modeling, advising, or coaching. Research on mentoring programs finds that *self-esteem is boosted* when one person shows interest in another person. There are many formats for mentoring programs, including, school-based mentoring and programs offered by private non-profit organizations (e.g. Big Brother/Big Sisters, Boys and Girls Club) as well as state agencies. You are advised to recommend that your socially anxious young clients connect with a mentoring program if you sense that this form of support could improve self-esteem and relationship skills.

Selective Mutism

Selective mutism was only recently recognized as an anxiety-based condition when it was added to the anxiety disorders to the *DSM-5* in 2013. Selective mutism is best understood as a variation of social anxiety and it is most commonly observed in young children. Typically, children with this form of anxiety exhibit normal speech and language skills at home but do not participate verbally in other situations, such as school.

The following criteria must be met for a diagnosis of selective mutism:

- Consistent failure to speak in social situations where verbal communication is expected, such as in school

- Duration of at least one month (but not the first month of school)

- The condition interferes with educational or occupational achievement

Treatment for Selective Mutism

Effective psychotherapy for selective mutism addresses the anxiety that underlies the child's inability to speak in certain situations. Some children with selective mutism also benefit from speech-language therapy, occupational therapy, sensory-integration therapy, and other interventions that may be recommended by the main treatment provider.

Behavior therapy is the most effective approach with young children exhibiting selective mutism. This approach consists of a step-by-step plan where the child gradually engages in difficult speaking-type behaviors, as well a system of positive reinforcement whenever the child is able to accomplish those behaviors. The following specific components have proven effective when used together:

- *Contingency management* involves rewarding nonverbal communication such as pointing and whispering.

- *Shaping reinforcement* is provided for approximations of the target verbal behaviors (e.g., mouthing words, whispering, talking on the telephone) and later for normal speech. A reinforcement menu (what types of rewards the child wants to earn and for what behaviors) is first developed in collaboration with the child.

- *Stimulus fading* interventions build on the success of contingency management and shaping by gradually increasing the number of people and places in which speech is rewarded. For example, the child may first be rewarded for speaking to a classmate to whom s/he already speaks outside of school. Gradually, other students are introduced until the child is able to speak in the presence of a large group of peers. Stimulus fading can also be used in problematic situations that occur outside of school (e.g. talking to grandparents, ordering in fast food restaurants).

- *Systematic desensitization* traditionally involves the use of relaxation skills along with gradual exposure to successively more anxiety-provoking situations. In this type of intervention, a hierarchy of feared speaking events is constructed and therapy consists of a series of visualized and real-life exposures to feared situations.

- *Social skills* training is appropriate to reduce anxiety and facilitate speech with peers and involves learning what to say to initiate conversations, how to take turns, making eye contact, and learning how to understand another person's nonverbal behavior.

- *Self-modeling* involves making video clips and/or audio recordings edited to depict the child speaking in settings in which he or she has previously remained mute. The recordings are played repeatedly throughout the intervention, with the expectation that the child will begin to believe in his or her ability to communicate verbally.

Effective psychotherapy also includes a cognitive focus that addresses the thoughts behind the speaking avoidance. Introducing cognitive strategies is most useful for children age 7 and older, when they have developed the ability to become aware of their thoughts. Techniques include recognizing body symptoms of anxiety, identifying and challenging maladaptive beliefs, and developing a coping plan to deal with distress. For example, many selectively mute children have anxious thoughts or worries that people will make fun of their voice or what they want to say. Cognitive therapy teaches the child client to understand that those thoughts are the product of worry (and are not real threats) and to coach themselves to replace worry with positive thoughts, such as:

- "I am a nice and capable person."

- "I am brave and I will talk in school when I am ready."

- "I am safe in school and my teacher will protect me if necessary."

Other therapies commonly used alongside the behavioral or cognitive-behavioral strategies described above are aimed at increasing the child's self-esteem. Improved self-esteem can strengthen the child emotionally by reinforcing areas of competence, belonging and acceptance as he or she completes the difficult work involved in these behavioral and cognitive-behavioral therapies. These may include learning new skills and/or encouraging participating in sports, music, arts, etc. The self-esteem strategies described earlier in this chapter for treating social anxiety are appropriate for selective mutism and can be adapted for use with young children.

Speech-language pathologists (SLPs) may contribute importantly to the treatment of children with selective mutism, since speech and/or language impairments can co-occur with this anxiety disorder. SLPs are trained in working with pragmatic language that can be significantly impacted in children with selective mutism. For these children, simultaneous treatment using both behavioral strategies to help them feel more comfortable speaking and linguistically based activities to foster language development is the best practice.

Specific Phobia

Whereas social phobia is recognized as a separate anxiety disorder, specific phobia refers to all other situations or things that trigger fear or anxiety. There are many objects or situations that can provoke anxiety, and they are highly individualized. As with most forms of anxiety, the reaction is out of proportion to actual danger or threat and, therefore, specific phobias are largely a matter of perception. On the other hand, there seem to be some situations that naturally activate fear in children, and even adults, such as thunder and lighting, darkness and insects. The *DSM-5* places specific phobias into several groups, each of which has its own sub-code. The groups are:

- Animals (e.g. insects, dogs)
- Natural environment (e.g. heights, storms, water)
- Blood-injection-injury (e.g. needles, invasive medical procedures)
- Situational (e.g. airplanes, elevators, enclosed spaces)
- Other (situations that might lead to choking or vomiting, and in young children, loud noises or costumed characters)

These are the criteria that must be met for a diagnosis of specific phobia:

- An immediate fear or anxiety in response to a specific object or situation.
- The phobic object or situation is either avoided or endured with intense fear or anxiety.
- The fear or anxiety is out of proportion to actual danger posed by the object or situation.
- The fear or anxiety causes distress or impairment in social, academic or other important areas of functioning.
- The pattern of fear or anxiety has lasted for at least 6 months.
- In children, crying, tantrums, freezing or clinging may express the anxiety.

Treatment for Specific Phobias

The most effective approach for specific phobias consists of exposure therapy. In introducing this approach to young children it might be helpful to coach the explanation in terms of being "scientists." You can explain exposure as controlled "experiments" about the child's fear and how to better help the child face the fear and learn how to handle the associated feelings and thoughts.

When feasible, in vivo exposure using real-life stimuli is the most efficient intervention and it has three main purposes:

1. Exposure is a mechanism for eliciting fear so that catastrophic cognitions and expectancies can be activated and addressed.
2. Exposure permits fear to habituate and avoidance to extinguish.
3. Exposure prevents behavioral and cognitive avoidance in a safe and controlled environment.

Exposure is carried out as a series of negotiated behavioral "experiments" based on a fear hierarchy and catastrophic cognitions obtained in earlier sessions of therapy. The child must understand that in order for therapy to be effective he or she might experience moderate levels of fear. On the other hand, when using exposure therapy with children it is important to give them appropriate control over the pace of the process. Keep in mind that the trust level and rapport you develop with a child will influence the amount of risk they are willing to take during exposure.

It is important to move sensitively and gradually towards *in vivo* exposure and, therefore, it is sometimes necessary to begin with a *virtual reality stimulus*. This step consists of using photographs, Internet research, sound recordings or other stimuli that are realistic enough to evoke the anxiety but which are not the actual feared object or situation. This is the essence of graduated exposure and it will be up to your judgment and creativity to determine the steps towards in vivo exposure.

As an example, a child with dog phobia can be helped using an exposure therapy process that begins with photographs and discussion about dogs. Film clips with friendly dog scenes could be used during this phase. When appropriate and feasible, a real dog can be introduced into a setting with therapist and child. The exposure sequence might then follow these steps:

Sample Exposure Therapy for Dog Phobia

1. A small dog is brought into the room leashed by an assistant who holds the leash close and tight at the opposite end of the room from the child and clinician. The clinician encourages the child to watch the dog and praises progress. They discuss how the dog's behavior is similar or dissimilar to expectations and cognitions discussed earlier.
2. The clinician suggests moving closer. If the child declines, the interim is used to discuss educational elements regarding dogs (e.g., "*Do you know how to tell a mean dog from a nice dog? How can we tell if that is a mean or nice dog?*"). The clinician again suggests moving closer. The child and clinician might then move several feet closer to the dog and discuss/challenge cognitions.
3. The clinician again suggests moving closer but offers reassurance and praise for any forward movement.
4. The clinician suggests allowing the dog 2 more feet of freedom on its retractable leash.
5. The child agrees to allow the clinician to touch the dog. Predictions of what will happen are discussed.
6. The clinician encourages the child to move closer while the clinician pets the dog.
7. The clinician praises the child's movement toward the dog until the child is independently petting the leashed dog.
8. The clinician assesses any catastrophic thought (e.g., "*it will bite me*") and asks the child for a prediction of what will happen if he or she pets the dog's head. With permission, the clinician demonstrates how the dog dislikes having the clinician's hand in its mouth. The child is then encouraged to do the same and performance is discussed.
9. Exposure continues until treatment is completed.
10. Similar steps could be taken with second and third dogs increasing in size. The process could continue until sufficient behavioral experiments have been conducted and until the child exhibits little or no anxiety in the presence of dogs.

Tests in school—subject quizzes as well as standardized achievement tests—are anxiety arousing for up to 41% of all students (Turner, Beidel, Hughs & Turner, 1993). The prevalence is difficult to determine due to discrepancies in how test anxiety is defined and inconsistencies in measuring how it affects performance. What seems clear, however, is that a significant percentage of students (25-30% as reported by Hill & Wigfield, 1984) suffer from crippling anxiety in test and evaluation situations that lowers their performance. In those cases, tests may not be a valid measure of their knowledge or ability. Test anxiety can be considered a specific phobia that can generalize beyond poor test performance and lead to lower academic achievement, behavior problems, school refusal and becoming turned off to learning.

Treatment for test anxiety consists of a combination of anxiety reduction practice and learning test-taking skills. For the anxiety reduction component, draw from the menu of relaxation practices described in Chapter 3. For improving test-taking skills, the following handout can be used with children and adolescents.

Managing Test Anxiety

Test anxiety is a specific phobia whose symptoms interfere with concentration, problem solving and creative thinking. Symptoms can include excessive or unreasonable fear, tension, apprehension and somatic arousal before, during or after an examination. In most cases, test anxiety is associated with excessive concerns about performance as well as "fear of anxiety symptoms." Avoiding tests is usually not a realistic coping option. Test anxiety varies in intensity from normal (experienced by most people but does not impair performance) to a debilitating anxiety disorder.

Before tests:

- Prepare and study in advance
- Develop good study skills
- Make and use flash cards
- Take good notes
- Make outlines and summaries
- Participate in study groups
- Use school resource centers if available for study tips, tutoring and other supports
- Learn and practice relaxation skills (see Chapter 3)
- Develop a healthy life-style including proper diet, exercise and adequate sleep (see Chapter 3)
- Visualize yourself doing well on tests
- Practice positive self-talk regarding the test
- Avoid talking about exams immediately before test-'taking if it raises anxiety level
- Be familiar with test time and location
- Limit worrying to a pre-determined "worry time" and say "not now" at other times
- Prepare the night before and collect any items you will need to take to the exam

During tests:

- Sit where you will have minimum distractions
- Carefully read any test instructions
- Scan the test and plan your approach
- Move on from difficult items instead of losing valuable time or going blank
- Focus on the test and stay in the here-and-now
- Avoid comparing your progress to other peoples'. Use relaxation skills to counteract tension or worry

Special accommodations for severe cases:

- Extra time to complete tests
- Alternative locations for test taking to minimize distractions and reduce anxiety
- Alternative assessment methods, such as written essays or take-home exams
- Tutoring in weak subject areas

Trauma and Stressor-Related Disorders

In the *DSM-5*, the posttraumatic stress disorder (PTSD) category was expanded to include attachment disorders and adjustment disorders. In doing so, the American Psychiatric Association focused on the role of stress as a source of anxiety. This concept is consistent with the framework presented earlier in this book, in which stress is considered the "when" factor in anxiety. In that framework, stress is the condition under which anxiety symptoms emerge in people who are predisposed to anxiety by their biological sensitivity and personality style. Stress, then, is the unifying concept in this expanded anxiety category.

However, the trauma-and stress-related disorders are separated from the anxiety disorders in the *DSM-5*. It is beyond the scope of this child anxiety treatment guide to address attachment disorders and adjustment disorders. We will focus only on the traditionally recognized form of trauma-based anxiety—posttraumatic stress disorder.

The essential feature of posttraumatic stress disorder (PTSD) is the development of anxiety symptoms following exposure to one or more traumatic events. Such symptoms vary widely and can include autonomic over-reactivity, such as nightmares, flashbacks, hyper-vigilance, tension, agitation, disorganization, and repetitive trauma reenactment in children's play. But symptoms may also include autonomic under-reactivity, such as depression, withdrawal, emotional detachment and sleep issues.

Traumatic events are defined as any event in which a person experienced, witnessed or was confronted with actual or threatened death or injury, or threat to the physical integrity of self or others. With children, such events include witnessing violence perpetrated on a family member or another person, inappropriate sexual experiences without physical violence or injury, sexual abuse, physical abuse, being kidnapped, natural disasters (e.g. hurricanes, floods) and man-made disasters or accidents (e.g. house fire, automobile accident involving injury to self or others). In young children, trauma can include learning that a traumatic event occurred to a parent or caregiver. When trauma-related anxiety symptoms are evident within 30 days of exposure to a traumatic event, the diagnosis of acute stress disorder is appropriate.

The following symptoms lasting more than a month suggest a diagnosis of PTSD:

- Recurrent, involuntary or intrusive distressing memories or dreams of the traumatic event (in children older than 6 play in which trauma themes are evident)

- Intense psychological distress in response to memories, reminders or symbolic cues of the trauma

- Efforts to avoid or actual avoidance of reminders, thoughts, feelings or memories of the traumatic event

- Negative beliefs, such as self-blame or survivor guilt

- Depressive symptoms, such as withdrawal, detachment, or diminished interest/participation in significant activities

- Autonomic over-reactivity (e.g. hypervigilance, impaired concentration, irritability, sleep problems, exaggerated startle response, reckless or self-destructive behavior)

It is estimated that 50% of children and adolescents will experience at least one trauma by age 18. A 1998 study of 17,421 children, known as the Adverse Childhood Experiences Study (ACE) found that

64% had at least one abuse experience and 22% had three or more traumatic experiences (Felitti, 1998). Another large-scale study of 14,773 children found that 47% had witnessed violence and 48% had lost a caregiver (SAMHSA 2012). However, not all children who have experienced adverse or traumatic events develop PTSD. Some manifest the effects of trauma with other types of symptoms including attention deficit disorders, mood disorders and behavior disorders. The response to trauma seems to vary by age range: preschool children are more likely to act out aggressively, school age children are more likely to exhibit mood disturbances such as depression, and teens are more likely to exhibit anxiety symptoms and social isolation.

Treatment for PTSD

If you are working with a child and adolescent within 30 days of their exposure to a traumatic event and they are exhibiting symptoms of anxiety, the condition is referred to as acute stress disorder. In such cases, your role is crisis intervention with the following strategies and goals:

- Get the facts
- Ensure safety
- Normalize feelings (e.g. fear, confusion, anger)
- Use a group format if possible for common experience (e.g. school shooting, natural disaster)

These steps may be helpful in mitigating the likelihood of developing an anxiety disorder such as PTSD.

After 30 days, the goal of therapy for PTSD is to help clients tolerate and ultimately reduce the anxiety symptoms that arise in response to trauma memories, reminders or cues. Talk therapy can be a form of exposure and desensitization to trauma memories but this format is often unsuccessful in reducing the anxiety. In many cases, therapy needs to address the somatic impact of trauma. Strategies to accomplish this task are discussed below. Nevertheless, it is important to initially help your child or adolescent client tell the story about what happened.

There are many tools and strategies for helping young clients tell their trauma story. Nonverbal forms of communication, such as drawing and sand tray with young children, or writing for adolescents can facilitate the story-telling process. Of course, verbal techniques such as use of puppets or mutual story telling are appropriate for children who are comfortable with and able to use language. While you may know the trauma history from discussions with a child's parents or other sources, it is important to understand the story and what it means from the child's perspective.

On the other hand, based on brain scans of adult volunteers it has been found that the brain area associated with verbal language can become inactive or inhibited during traumatic emotional memories (van der Kolk, 2014). With children, talk therapy for trauma may also be problematic due to their limited verbal skills especially when then trauma history begins before language development. Nonverbal interventions may be necessary to help children heal from the impact of trauma.

It is now understood that the effects of trauma can become embedded in the body—in a neuromuscular "shock" response that can become a chronic state of physical tension. The normal survival response of freezing in response to threat can stay "on" and the associated neuromuscular tension does not readily release through verbal therapy. As a result, clients with trauma histories may feel numb or disconnected from their feelings and physical sensations. Therefore, it is often necessary to introduce somatic-focused interventions.

Somatic interventions are designed to help clients connect with and be comfortable in their bodies. Any activity or practice that can move clients in this direction should be explored. They include many of the activities described in Chapter 3. Here is a list of recommended activities for young people with PTSD:

- Yoga
- Martial arts (e.g. Aikido, T'ai chi, Karate)
- Dance
- Exercise, physical movement and outdoor recreational activities (see Chapter 3)
- Flow activities (see Chapter 3)
- Playing music and singing
- Breathing practices

If you are familiar with or qualified to teach any of these skills, you can capitalize on your positive relationship and credibility with your client by introducing these important self-help activities. As a role model you may also inspire them to practice something new that could be helpful in their recovery from trauma. For some clients, it may also help to refer to bodywork specialists, such as massage therapists, physical therapists and occupational therapists, who can provide somatic therapy services to help with trauma recovery.

A controversial issue in trauma therapy is "repressed memory." Just as the impact of trauma can affect the body, trauma can affect cognitive functioning, such as memory, attention and concentration. Trauma victims of all ages can develop "defensive amnesia" or memory loss that protects them from anxious feelings. In these cases trauma memories and associated feelings are not consciously accessible in therapy. This usually means that a client is not ready for direct discussion or processing of traumatic experiences.

When trauma-related feelings emerge, you may find clients "dissociating," feeling "numb" or 'leaving their bodies" during therapy sessions. When you find that a client is exhibiting any of these mechanisms, you are advised to slow down and postpone any interventions that might re-activate anxiety. It seems wise to move slowly in helping a client to shift from *telling* the trauma story to *feeling* or *re-experiencing* it. It is then appropriate to introduce relaxation skills to neutralize or soften any emotional pain that might arise when reconnecting to the body. This sequence requires time and patience so child therapists should be comfortable with a gradual and gentle process in PTSD cases.

Sometimes PTSD does not result from acute trauma but rather from long-term, chronic abuse and neglect. This chronic form of traumatic stress has been called "developmental trauma disorder" but the term has not yet been recognized in the *DSM-5*. In these cases, therapy is likely to require collateral services, such as child protective services and parenting educators, to ensure safety and address the family sources of stress and anxiety.

Beyond the family, children growing up in today's world are exposed to many other sources of potential PTSD. Terrorism, natural disasters, school shootings and violence in the media (video games, movies, television and even some music) are all potential sources of anxiety and PTSD. The media can vicariously traumatize children when it reports on violent and catastrophic global events. Even adults are exposed on a daily basis to trauma-inducing events, leading one psychiatrist to write a book entitled,

The Trauma of Everyday Life (Epstein, 2014). How can you guide parents, therapists and teachers to be helpful with children exposed to these sources of anxiety and PTSD? How can adults address real world threats and dangers without stimulating unnecessary or counter-productive anxiety in children? What advice can you give parents and teachers to counteract the potential PTSD in children exposed to tragedy, violence and disaster?

Here are some suggestions for adults to guide in processing children's exposure directly or indirectly to traumatic events:

Recommendations for Helping Children Cope with Trauma, Catastrophe and Disaster

- Keep in mind that reactions to trauma are a process that may manifest in different ways over time.

- Stay calm and collected, as children look to adults for safety signals.

- Take time to deal with your own reactions. Seek support and comfort if needed.

- Ask the child to tell you what he knows of the events. Use the child's level of understanding to steer your response.

- Encourage questions and discussion, and let a child's questions guide the content of the conversation.

- Answer questions honestly and accurately but limit information to necessary details.

- Use language appropriate to a child's developmental level using age-appropriate metaphors and analogies. Young children may benefit from play or drawings.

- Acknowledge and accept a child's fears, affirming that it is normal to feel upset, worried or angry.

- Share your own reactions to help normalize children's experience, but not to burden them.

- Reassure children that they are safe and protected. Older children and teenagers may benefit from knowing all the measures being taken to ensure their safety, whereas young children merely need to know that they are safe.

- Give children as many valid reasons as possible about why they are unlikely targets, but acknowledge that bad things sometimes do happen.

- When children push for guarantees about safety, acknowledge that absolute safety cannot be guaranteed. On the other hand, there is a difference between what is possible and what is probable.

- Parents should be physically and emotionally available to provide nurturing and comfort as needed.

- Make extra time to be with children at transition times (mornings, evenings and bedtime) to allow opportunities for questions and communication about feelings.

- Help the child distinguish between real and imagined fears.

- Teach children how to communicate distress and to ask for help when needed.
- Use a feeling thermometer as an index of emotional intensity and the effect of self-regulation skills.
- Limit exposure to media replays of traumatic events.
- Watch television with children to monitor exposure and respond to concerns.
- Avoid detailed adult discussions of the events in the presence of children.
- Focus on the facts and dispel misinformation and misconceptions.
- Model the behavior that children are expected to learn.
- Be aware of your own feelings and channel them appropriately.
- Teach children that anger and conflicts are best resolved with language rather than physically acting out.
- Resume normal family and school routines as soon as possible.
- Spend extra time doing enjoyable activities with children and refocus them away from anxiety.
- Maintain regular bedtime schedules, but provide extra comfort if needed such as a nightlight, special toys or sitting with the child until he falls asleep.
- Express optimism about returning to normalcy.
- Reduce feelings of helplessness by encouraging children to show caring and empathy for other victims by donating clothes or toys, collecting money for relief efforts, writing letters or attending a prayer service.
- Turn to your faith, family or friends when you need support or understanding.
- Children who are prone to anxiety can be expected to be more nervous, tearful, clingy, distractible or regressed following exposure to traumatic events.
- Therapy is recommended when a child's fears or distress are severe or continue for over a month.

Medication And Nature's Remedies

Since medication is an important option in treatment for anxiety, let us consider its advantages and disadvantages for children. My thoughts turn to medication when my young clients are experiencing any of the following conditions:

- Insomnia that does not resolve with sleep recommendations (see page 36)
- Symptoms so distracting, such as frequent panic attacks, that therapy is unproductive
- Significant depression or suicide potential

Under these conditions, a client's ability to benefit from therapy is compromised and a referral for a medication evaluation should be considered.

It is important to be sensitive to parents' feelings or value systems about medication. Some parents are simply opposed to drugs of any kind, including prescription medications, while other parents may seek your opinion about adding medication to the treatment plan. Children may also have strong feelings and concerns about taking medication. These should also be respected. In general, I recommend avoiding conflicts with clients and parents regarding medication, although it is appropriate to inquire about the basis of their feelings. In rare cases, when you feel that it is not safe to continue therapy without medication, such as with a suicidal client, you are within your rights to discontinue treatment so long as you make a responsible referral to another provider.

The advantages of medication include helping a child make the most of therapy. In this sense, medication serves as an adjunct to therapy and can be discontinued when clients acquire the skills that will enable them to manage their symptoms.

Medication can also play a role in the treatment of phobias, where a child's anxiety pattern is in response to a specific "threat." These can include school avoidance, social phobia, and public speaking. In such cases, the use of medication can help a child enter a feared situation in order to practice the anxiety-control skills learned in therapy.

Another role for medication is in treating the depression that often accompanies anxiety disorders. Depression is a natural consequence of anxiety, especially when the anxiety is chronic. For example, a child or adolescent with social phobia is likely to become depressed as a result of social isolation and loneliness. In such cases, the antidepressant medications—which have few troublesome side effects and are generally considered safe for children—can be an important component of therapy.

Many doctors prefer that patients with anxiety and depression be in therapy while they are on medication. This helps monitor any adverse medication side effects while enhancing the overall effectiveness of treatment.

But medications have several disadvantages and pitfalls. One is the bias against drugs that many parents and children have when they come for help. I have found that it is best to align with my patients when they have strong negative feelings against medication, even when I think it might be helpful. My strategy is to discuss the possible benefits of medication and suggest that we revisit the topic if therapy is unsuccessful after a reasonable period of time, such as 3 or 4 months.

> Recent evidence indicates that the use of SSRI medications, such as Paxil, with children may be unsafe. In 2003, the drug manufacturer GlaxoSmithKline, Inc. issued a warning that Paxil (paroxetine hydrochloride) should not be used with children or adolescents under the age of 18 "due to a possible increased risk of suicide-related adverse events in this patient population." The warning was based on placebo-controlled studies of children taking Paxil for social phobia, obsessive-compulsive disorder, and major depressive disorder. The studies revealed increased suicidal thinking and suicide attempts in children and adolescents (three times greater than in children taking a placebo). The drug warning suggests that children who are already using Paxil should discontinue by tapering off rather than stopping abruptly, preferably under medical supervision.

Another class of medications called benzodiazepines, such as Xanax, Klonopin, Valium, and Ativan, are considered effective for quick relief from anxiety in adults. However, these medications are considered unsafe for regular use with children.

Even without these safety concerns, another disadvantage is that the SSRI drugs most frequently used to treat anxiety in children are not immediately effective in most cases. They can take up to 4 weeks to achieve a therapeutic effect, which is too long for many impatient clients. In some cases, the opposite effect takes place: there is an initial increase in anxiety symptoms. And the process of finding the right medication at the right dosage, which can involve numerous visits to the prescribing psychiatrist or doctor, can be frustrating and time-consuming.

Medications do not teach children any new skills or help them understand their anxiety. Therefore, medication should be combined with therapy for maximum benefit from both. In fact, recent research indicates that the rate of anxiety relapse is high with medication alone, but that adding therapy to medication reduces the rate of anxiety relapse. Some other interesting research on the combination of medication and psychotherapy has been reported. It has been found that cognitive-behavioral therapy (CBT) alone may initially be more costly than medication, but by one year it is only half the cost of medication. Also, combining CBT and medication may enhance the effectiveness of CBT in the short run but it actually *reduces* its efficacy in the long run. With panic disorder, medication has been found to be equally effective as CBT, but relapse after treatment is more common with medication alone. And with OCD, it has been shown that CBT is as effective as medication in altering brain chemistry in the brain area (caudate nucleus) associated with unwanted thoughts and urges.

There is also an issue in some cases with psychological dependence on medications. This can be a significant problem, especially when a drug is effective at controlling anxiety symptoms. Indeed, I have worked with patients of all ages who came in with complaints about discontinuing their medication. They experienced a return of anxiety after they stopped taking medication. This introduces an additional therapy challenge: helping a client recover from use of medication.

Side effects of medication are a special problem in child anxiety cases because of biological sensitivity. The temperament of anxious children usually includes sensory sensitivity to a wide range of stimuli (e.g., lights, sounds, physical contact, certain foods, and hormone changes). This sensitivity factor can also apply to medications, possibly magnifying any adverse side effects. In my experience, anxious children and adults are more reactive than the general population to the side effects of medications.

Considering the fact that about 80% of children with anxiety disorders can benefit from therapy without medications, my opinion is that drugs should be used only when necessary and with an awareness of side effects and risks. Except for the two conditions mentioned earlier—inability to sleep and severe symptoms that interfere with counseling—I start with counseling and consider medication only if a reasonable effort is ineffective.

Below is a guide to the commonly used medications for anxiety in children. This guide displays the medication options and the anxiety disorders for which they are typically recommended.

Medicines For Anxiety Disorders In Children And Adolescents

FDA Approved

Luvox: OCD

Zoloft: OCD

Anafranil: OCD

Prozac: OCD

Limited Clinical Study Evidence

Buspar: GAD

Effexor XR: GAD, PD*

Luvox: GAD, SAD*

Paxil: GAD, SAD, PD, PTSD*

Prozac: PD, PTSD*

Zoloft: GAD, SAD, PTSD, Separation Anxiety*

Strattera: GAD, Social Anxiety, Separation Anxiety combined with ADHD

Anecdotal Use

Ativan: acute PD, Acute PTSR (adolescents)

Celexa, Lexapro: GAD, SAD, PTSD*

Clonidine, Guanfacine: Acute PTSR, PTSD (children and adolescents)

Klonopin: acute PD, PTSR (adolescents)

Xanax, Xanax XR: acute PD (adolescents)

*These medicines have new warning requirements regarding suicidal ideation in depression, not yet associated with anxiety disorder use. Close monitoring is advised due to co-morbidity issues.

Alternative-Medicine Approaches

There are some interesting alternative-medicine approaches that are applicable to children with anxiety disorders. Some are widely used in Europe, where they have a long history of use by medical doctors. Herbal preparations, for example, are regulated as medicines in Germany and France, where they are manufactured with strict quality controls. In those countries, medical training includes these forms of treatment.

In contrast, American medical practice has been slow to recognize the value of alternative or "natural" treatments, and many physicians are skeptical about their usefulness. Yet this is changing: Approximately two-thirds of the 125 medical schools in the United States have introduced some form of alternative or complementary medicine in their curriculums. Let us look at some of these alternative-medical approaches as they apply to children's anxiety.

Herbal Therapy

Herbs have been valued as remedies for nervousness, insomnia, and other anxiety symptoms since ancient times. Modern medical science, however, has only recently acknowledged their medicinal properties. Nevertheless, there has been a growing contemporary interest in herbs as part of a natural approach to health care, especially in response to dissatisfaction with the side effects of prescription drugs. The following brief review of herbs for anxiety is intended to orient readers to this option for children. However, this information should not be used as a substitute for guidance by a qualified health care provider.

The popularity of herbs has increased in part due to media coverage. In addition, health care in the United States is shifting to incorporate self-education and self-care. Herbal medicine seems to fit naturally into this new paradigm.

One problem with herbal preparations is that at present the U.S. Food and Drug Administration does not regulate them or consider them medicines. As a result, no official quality standards exist for herbs in the United States, and they must be sold as "supplements." Furthermore, current law prevents the labeling of herbs as capable of treating or preventing diseases or symptoms, although manufacturers can claim that their products enhance well-being or that they support or help improve body functions, so long as the claims are supported by scientific evidence.

Research in support of herbs for anxiety treatment is growing, but studies involving children are limited. Therefore, parents and others considering the use of herbs with children are advised to consult with knowledgeable professionals. This generally means naturopathic physicians (NDs) and alternative health-care professionals. Also, self-education about herbs for anxiety in children is recommended. As a general rule, herbal remedies should not be combined with prescription drugs because of potentially adverse interaction effects.

Chamomile has a long history as a calming agent and is widely used for anxiety and insomnia. There is ample anecdotal support for its safety and effectiveness with children but inconclusive scientific evidence. When my own children were young, I sometimes used a chamomile blend as a warm, soothing drink when they had difficulty falling asleep. I created a calming ritual in which I took the tea to them in their special cups and talked with them in bed while they sipped. Perhaps the combination of reassuring attention and the calming effect of the herb was responsible for the positive effect.

Other herbs that have been used with children include St. John's wort, hops, passionflower, skullcap, valerian, and oat straw. The choice of herbs will usually depend on what symptoms are targeted. For example, St. John's wort is typically used for daytime calming, while valerian is used as a sedative for sleep. In addition, some practical considerations may be involved. For example, children can be picky about what they will eat or drink, and the taste of an herbal tea may determine whether it will be tolerated. Chamomile, kava, St. John's wort, and passionflower have mild tastes that are acceptable to most children.

Aromatherapy

Related to herbal medicines, aromatherapy is a system of healing using aromatic essences of plant extracts called *essential oils*. The oils evaporate at room temperature or when warmed. Essential oils have been used for health purposes, including relaxation and tension reduction, for thousands of years, dating back to ancient Egypt and China.

Aromas act directly on the brain through nerve receptors in the nose. Millions of nerve cells in our nasal passageways send impulses to the hypothalamus and limbic areas—the brain's emotional centers. The sense of smell is so powerfully connected to the brain that some odors can elicit vivid memories.

Pleasant fragrances prompt us to take slower, deeper breaths that induce relaxation. The scent of lavender, for example, is associated with increased alpha brain waves (relaxed brain waves). In a study reported in *Lancet*, the prestigious British medical journal, lavender was found to reduce anxiety and induce sleep in subjects with insomnia. Other soothing essential oils include chamomile, neroli, bergamot, sweet marjoram, and ylang-ylang, which can be used individually or in combination for stress relief. Some of these fragrances have also been used to calm hyperactive children.

Using essential oils is as simple as smelling the oils from the bottle or applying a few drops to the hands or wrists. However, since some oils may cause irritation to the skin, it is recommended that they be diluted with a carrier oil, such as sweet almond, olive, safflower, or sesame seed. Due to the high concentration of essential oils, one source recommends a mix consisting of 10 % essential oil and 90 % carrier oil. For longer-lasting scents, scent dispensers, aroma lamps, or electric aromatherapy oil diffusers are commercially available.

It is recommended that essential oils be purchased from a manufacturer of pure plant oils. Many essential oils on the market are adulterated or diluted with synthetic or less expensive but impure oils. Perfume or fragrance oils are almost always synthetic, with no therapeutic benefits. Cosmetic companies, in particular, carry synthetic oils that are not recommended for aromatherapy.

Homeopathy

Like herbal therapy, homeopathy is an alternative healing science that often uses natural plant remedies. One crucial difference, however, is that homeopathy involves carefully prepared and administered substances that may have adverse effects in large quantities but that stimulate self-healing and balance in very minute dosages. Another difference is that homeopathic medicines are defined and regulated as drugs by the FDA.

Homeopathic remedies are prepared through a process called *potentization*—a series of shaking actions. This procedure reportedly removes all risk of chemical toxicity while activating a remedy substance and enabling it to affect the body therapeutically.

Homeopathic remedies are usually selected based on a close match with the target symptoms, and unless otherwise specified by the physician, they can be taken according to instructions printed on the label. Some examples of homeopathic remedies for anxiety are:

Remedies used for anxiety In children

Aconitum napellus — Used for acute anxiety, bad dreams, and sleep problems in children.

Pulsatilla — Children who express anxiety as insecurity and clinginess, with a need for constant support and comforting, may benefit from this remedy. Anxiety around the time of hormonal changes (puberty, menstrual periods) often is helped with pulsatilla.

Gelsemium — Feelings of weakness, trembling, or feeling "paralyzed by fear" suggest this remedy. It is considered helpful for test anxiety, a visit to the dentist, stage fright before a public performance or interview, or other stressful event.

Natrum muriaticum — Emotional sensitivity, self-protective shy- ness, and social phobia are indications for this remedy. Claustrophobia, anxiety at night (with fears of robbers or intruders), migraines, and insomnia may also be helped with the remedy.

Phosphorus — This remedy is prescribed for people who are open- hearted, imaginative, excitable, easily startled, and full of intense and vivid fears. Also appropriate for some of the anxiety personality traits, such as a tendency to overextend oneself, suggestibility, habitual worry, and negative thinking.

Since homeopathic drug products must be chosen on a case-by-case basis, use of these remedies with children should be done only in consultation with a trained homeopathic physician. Homeopathic doctors can be located in local directories under "Naturopathic Physicians." Below is an annotated resource list of organizations promoting the alternative medicine approaches discussed in this chapter.

Resources for Complimentary and Alternative Medicine

www.kidshealth.org/en/parents/alternative-medicine.html# (article on alternative medicine for children in KidsHealth)

www.nccih.nih.gov/health/integrative-health (National Center for Complimentary and Integrative Health at the National Institute of Health is the U.S. government's leading agency for scientific research on complementary and integrative health care)

www.ahha.org (American Holistic Health Association offers free and impartial information about holistic health care)

www.mdanderson.org/departments/cimer (Complementary/Integrative Medicine Education Resources provides educational resources to health care professionals and the public about the current understanding of complementary medicine)

www.faim.org (Foundation for Alternative and Integrative Medicine offers research reports on the effectiveness of alternative medicines)

Herbs

www.herbalgram.org/ (American Botanical Council, also known as the Herbal Medicine Institute, is an independent, nonprofit research and education organization dedicated to providing accurate and reliable information for consumers, healthcare practitioners, researchers, educators, industry and the media)

www.americanherbalistsguild.com (American Herbalists Guild supports access to herbal medicine for all and advocates excellence in herbal education)

www.herbs.org (Herb Research Foundation offers information based on "solid science and informed opinion" about herbs as well as complimentary and alternative health care)

www.herbsociety.org (Herb Society of America is dedicated to promoting the knowledge and use of herbs through educational programs and research)

Homoeopathy

www.homeopathyusa.org (American Institute o Homeopathy is the trade association of licensed alternative health care practitioners promoting homeopathy as a medical specialty)

www.homeopathycenter.org (National Center for Homeopathy offers a resource library as well as a national listing of homeopathic practitioners)

Aromatherapy

www.flowersociety.org (Flower Essence Society is an international membership organization of health practitioners, researchers and others interested in flower essence therapy, and has a section on use with children)

www.naha.org (National Association of Holistic Aromatherapists offers links to various websites that provide information on aromatherapy and related topics that are mainly noncommercial, as well as listing of aromatherapists)

Involving Parents In Child Therapy

Therapeutic Alliance with Parents

Virginia Satir, considered to be a pioneer in family therapy, recognized that effective work with children requires credibility with, and support from, the parents. Satir (1983a; 1983b) suggested that when there is conflict between a child's therapist and the child's parents, the parents will invariably prevail simply because they have more influence. To maximize parent support she advised therapists to develop a "therapeutic alliance" with parents. What did she mean and how can you develop a therapeutic alliance with parents?

It is almost always preferable for child therapists to begin by accepting a parent's definition of the problem, even when the parent is "blaming" the child for the problem. Most therapists who work with children and families take a "family systems" view of their cases and look at the dynamics and roles that each family member plays in the system. Frequently, the child is the *identified patient* or *symptom* in a dysfunctional family. For example, a child exhibiting separation anxiety may be reflecting unconsciously a parent's difficulty letting go. A child with a reactive attachment disorder (now classified as an anxiety disorder) may be a symptom in a family with a parent who is "out of tune" with the child or deficient in bonding capacity. A child exhibiting posttraumatic stress disorder may be a symptom of abuse or negligence within the family.

Unless you are dealing with reportable parental abuse or neglect, it is advisable to begin by forming an alliance with the parent(s). This is especially important when the parent rather than another party (such as a school guidance counselor or pediatrician) initiates therapy. A parent who initiates therapy is asking for help, and it would be counter-productive to start therapy by pointing out the parent's deficiencies or contribution to the problem.

Once you develop rapport and credibility with the parents, you can begin to influence the parents through the relationship you have developed. You can make suggestions and recommendations that are designed to support the child's progress in therapy. Parents are more likely to accept your advice and follow through on your recommendations when they have confidence in you and your work. Such confidence flows from the parent's sense that you understand and empathize with their experience. Some parents will go so far as to ask if *you* have children because they need to know that you can identify with their experience, and with what's it is like to have an anxious or otherwise symptomatic child.

Involving Parents in Therapy

You can involve parents in therapy in several ways. One is to begin the intake process with a parent interview without the child present. This allows time to listen to the parents and instill confidence that you understand their views of the problem and its history. You can follow up with periodic "parent conferences." These are separately scheduled sessions to confer with the parents and work collaboratively towards progress and change. Many therapists also spend a few minutes with parents before or at the end of the child's therapy sessions. This provides an opportunity for updates and communication about progress and change. This also helps to ensure that the parents are in tune with the therapy.

There are some important nuances in the therapeutic alliance with parents of adolescent clients. In such cases the challenge is to balance confidentiality of the information revealed in therapy with the parent's right to know. It would be helpful to negotiate the boundaries of confidentiality at the outset of therapy. Most parents will accept the need for confidentiality as a condition for effective counseling if they are assured that they will be informed of any high risk behavior. The adolescent would need to agree that there are certain conditions under which parents need to be informed, and these conditions should be spelled out. They include risk of self-harm, dangerous behavior such as drinking and driving (or use of any drugs and driving), unprotected sex, or credible threats of harm to others. Once this agreement is made the adolescent has the option of withholding information that he or she does not want the parent to know, although this is not in the best interests of therapy. I find that it works best when high risk behavior is revealed to tell the adolescent that one way or another the parents need to be informed, and ask the adolescent how he or she would like to handle it.

Managing Risks with Divorce Cases

Roughly half of married couples with children end in divorce, and half of those divorces are between parents with children under 18 years of age. According to projections based on 1990 census data, 40% of all children can expect to live in a single-parent household before the age of 16 because of divorce (Cherlin, 1992). A little math suggests that approximately one in three child and adolescent clients live in what has been called "binuclear families," or two-home families.

Working with children whose parents are divorced involves a number of potential ethical conduct and malpractice risks. The risks include multiple relationship complaints when called to render opinions about the best interests of child clients. Another risk consists of attempts by a bitter parent to sabotage your work or harass you when that person feels disempowered by the other parent who may have initiated therapy with you. In this section, I offer some recommendations to minimize such risks. First, let's look at the dynamics in post-divorce co-parenting to see what interventions and recommendations might help counteract the negative effects on children as well as minimize the risks for therapists.

The most comprehensive research on the effects of divorce on children was a 30-year longitudinal study by Wallerstein and Blakeslee (2003). In this study, a sample of 131 children and their divorcing parents was evaluated with psychological tests at the outset and then interviewed annually over a 30-year period. This research found that the most significant source of anxiety in children of divorce was *not* the stress at the time of separation and divorce but rather the quality of the ongoing coparenting relationship between the divorced parents, which may last for years.

Four types of co-parenting styles after divorce were identified and it should be obvious which of them are most effective at reducing anxiety in the children. The four co-parenting styles are:

Co-Parenting Styles in Divorced Parents

"Perfect pals" These are co-parents who share decision making and child rearing. They respect each other and are capable of doing family activities together. They may even maintain their friendship with each other. As a psychologist, I have had the good fortune of working with some families where this style was evident.

"Cooperative colleagues" While not friends with each other, these co-parents can work together for the sake of their children. They communicate amicably, share parenting responsibilities, and control their feelings and underlying conflicts.

"Angry associates" Adversarial battles and ongoing anger are characteristic of these co-parents after divorce. In this type of relationship, there are frequent conflicts around custody and visitations. Children in these families are more likely to exhibit anxiety, including a resurgence in their twenties when dealing with issues of commitment, marriage and whether to have children of their own.

"Fiery foes" In this hostile relationship, the ex-spouses have no capacity for cooperation as parents. They are the parents whose battles return to court because they are unable to communicate with each other. As in the case of "angry associates," children in these families tend to have more anxiety symptoms.

Naturally, parents who cannot get along while married are likely to have difficulty cooperating after divorce. While becoming "perfect pals" might be unrealistic in many cases, becoming "cooperative colleagues" is achievable. Cooperation after divorce is an important goal for reducing anxiety in children.

Below are some recommendations you can make to divorced parents to foster cooperation.

Recommendations for Divorced Parents

- Focus on your children's needs for peace, stability, and minimal loss.
- Recognize that your child's well-being requires a cooperative partnership with your ex-spouse.
- Seek personal therapy, if necessary, to let go of any anger, bitterness, or hurt that stands in the way of cooperative co-parenting.
- Learn conflict resolution skills, if necessary, to learn to communicate cooperatively with your ex-spouse.
- In your new relationships, seek support for your efforts to be cooperative with your ex-spouse.
- Do not use your child as a messenger for communicating with your ex-spouse
- Communicate directly with your ex-spouse by phone, e-mail or text and out of range of your child.
- Think ahead before you talk with your ex-spouse, and choose times when you are relaxed rather than stressed, hungry, or tired.
- If necessary, use a facilitator to keep communication cooperative and focused on the children's best interests.
- The legal system is adversarial and can reinforce a "win-lose" attitude. Try to resolve differences out of court, as arrangements are more likely to succeed if both parties are in agreement.
- If your ex-spouse cannot be won over to the idea of cooperation, stay on the high road of civility and self-control, and trust that your child will be better off for your efforts.

One step you can take to protect yourself is to ensure that you know which parent has legal authority to consent to treatment for the child. Parents are not always reliable or clear about their legal rights and responsibilities. Therefore, it is recommended that you ask for a copy of the divorce stipulation as it pertains to both legal rights and responsibilities and custody. Family courts have issued some complicated and unworkable stipulations, especially in high-conflict cases, such as awarding sole legal rights and responsibilities to one parent and joint custody for both parents. In such cases, one parent may feel disempowered and may act out by not supporting therapy or by insisting on access to the therapist or child's records. Even more problematic is that in most states the courts authorize parents without legal rights and responsibilities to have access to the records and to the child's therapist.

Here are some steps you can take to minimize complaints and problems in divorce cases:

1. Have both parents sign consent-to-treatment forms
2. Have both parents sign a policy statement that makes it clear you will not testify in any legal or court matters. Emphasize that you are providing therapy services, not a forensic evaluation, and that your role is specific to this purpose.
3. Know how to deal with subpoenas from attorneys or courts. A pre-emptive consultation with an attorney to acquire this information is a good investment if your practice includes children with divorced or separated parents.
4. Attend continuing education workshops on ethics, multiple relationships and risk management. Many states require 6 hours of such education for each license renewal period.

Keep in mind that most malpractice complaints against therapists are made by clients who are angry or who do not like the therapist, even when the therapist is doing effective work. Conversely, clients who like their therapist are unlikely to file malpractice complaints even when the therapist may not be doing effective work. These facts suggest, once again, that a positive therapeutic alliance with parents is key to successful work as well as risk management.

The impact of divorce on children can include stress, confusion, sadness, anxiety, loyalty conflicts, guilt and shame. How can you address these feelings and issues directly in your work with children? What concepts and language are appropriate and helpful?

Here is a script that you can use to address such feelings, especially anxiety, that may be occurring in children of divorce. I begin with a self-disclosure that you can omit if it does not apply to you as a therapist.

Language for Discussing Divorce with Children

> *When I was ten years old, my parents separated and then divorced. Like most children whose parents get divorced, I did not like the change because it made me feel sad, confused and anxious.*

> *Divorce can make children have anxiety for several reasons. One reason is fear that you will lose one or even both of your parents. That is really scary because as a child you depend on your parents. Unfortunately, in some divorce cases one parent does go away or become less involved. But that only happens some of the time. And no matter what, usually at least one parent continues to take good care of the children.*

Divorce is stressful for every member of the family. Parents might be upset or angry, and children may change schools or move to another house. Sometimes children go back and forth between two houses. That can be confusing and stressful.

Sometimes divorced parents say bad things about each other, or tell you things you don't want to hear. If this happens, you may need to tell your parents that it makes you uncomfortable when they talk like that. You can say, 'Mom (or Dad), it makes me feel uncomfortable, like I have to choose between my parents, when you talk like that.' If it continues, you could say, 'Dad (or Mom), I would appreciate it if you did not tell me things like that.' It would be better for your parents to have another adult to talk to about their feelings regarding the divorce.

The most important thing is for you to know that it is not your fault if your parents get divorced. Parents get divorced for many different reasons—maybe because they fight too much, or stop loving each other—but rarely because the children were bad and rarely because parents stop loving their children.

The best way for families to handle divorce is for both parents to continue to love and take care of you. You should be able to have a good relationship with both parents without feeling guilty or anxious. You can talk with me about your feelings if this is not happening in your family.

Also remember that not all love relationships end in divorce. When you get older and have your own love relationship, don't expect it to end. But take your time and make sure it's the right relationship before you make a commitment to get married or have children.

In Closing

I end this therapist's guidebook with a point made at the beginning and at several points throughout: effective therapy rests heavily on the quality of the therapist-client relationship. While this book offers many strategies, interventions, and skills, these tools will be most effective when used by therapists who can develop rapport, trust, and credibility with their child and adolescent clients.

Research on therapy outcomes finds that only 15% of therapy effectiveness is attributable to *technique*—the tools used by the therapist (Wampold, 2008; Lambert, 1992). Using a tool analogy, an unskilled carpenter with the best and newest tools will not do a good job. The most significant variable in therapy effectiveness is a combination of the *therapeutic relationship* (30%) and *therapist expectancy* (15%). Therapist expectancy is the therapist's belief, based on experience, in a client's ability to change and improve.

Your clients need to feel known and understood. They need to feel that you "get them," that you understand deeply and emotionally what it's like for them. How do you convey empathy for what it is like to be controlled by irrational obsessions and compulsive behavior, to feel attacked by panic anxiety, to suffer post-traumatic anxiety, to have difficulty sleeping or feel depressed due to frequent worry, or to be uncomfortable and anxious around other people? What does it take to connect with young people and establish the rapport, trust and credibility required for effective therapy?

Here are the qualities that seem to be needed for cultivating a positive and healing relationship with child and adolescent clients:

- Genuine interest in children
- Engaging, playful, fun
- Spontaneous and inventive
- Willing to learn from children
- Able to provide *active* learning experiences
- Contemporary and "cool" but not fake
- Able to *narrate* (think out loud) to convey coping strategies

Unfortunately, some of these qualities cannot be taught. You either have them or you do not have them. Children seem to know intuitively who gets them and who they can be trust. As one writer puts it, "Children have an uncanny x-ray vision and reject well-meaning but patronizing approaches (House, 2000)."

Remember also a point that was made in Chapter 2, that to work effectively with children you must also have a positive relationship with their parents. You must be able to shift gears between your child therapist role and your role with parents, in which you talk *about* your work with their children while also influencing the parents to change their own behavior to help their children. In other words, you have at least two clients when you work with children. In some cases, you will find yourself working on behalf of your child client when you are communicating with other adults involved—in schools, pediatrician offices and social service agencies. This requires flexibility, good communication skills, credibility and relationship skills with both children and adults.

The Center for Anxiety Disorders in Burlington, Vermont, where I serve as the director, has provider contracts with various health insurance companies that pay for therapy services. Some of the insurance companies analyze our billing claims and provide feedback on treatment patterns. The data that I am most proud of is our *engagement rate*. Engagement rate is defined as the *percentage of clients who return for therapy after their first appointment*. Based on our billing claims, we have a higher than state and national average engagement rate. This finding reflects our emphasis on the therapeutic relationship: we spend time in the first few therapy sessions developing rapport, trust and credibility with each client. I attribute a 15-year steady growth in our referral rate, staff size and income to this one simple value—that a positive therapist-client relationship is the key to success.

You are encouraged to use the information and interventions described in this book. You are also encouraged to experiment, refine and develop your own variations. In the age of manualized therapy protocols and pressure from health insurance companies for cost-effective quick fixes and short-term treatment, some therapists feel that they can no longer invest time in developing a therapeutic relationship or be creative with therapy interventions. You are advised to be yourself and find your own way to implement what you find in this book. If not, you are likely to be less effective, as expressed in this final thought:

"Despite the fact that many of the best empirically-based practices are effective, most veterans of psychotherapy know that one of the most important aspects of psychotherapeutic treatment is the personality, style and spontaneity of the therapist. Following treatment manuals has, unfortunately, left some therapists believing that they 'can't color outside the box' and do things once considered innovative because it might deviate from the empirically-based treatment protocol and risk violating the standard of care." (Datillo, 2006).

With all the best wishes for applying the ideas and strategies in this guidebook and for being creative and innovative in developing your own way of delivering them,

Paul Foxman, Ph.D.

Readings and References

For your convenience, you may download a PDF version of the handouts in this book from our dedicated website: go.pesi.com/foxman

Aron, E. *The Highly Sensitive Child.* New York: Broadway Books (Random House), 2004.

Baptiste, B. *My Daddy is a Pretzel: Yoga for Parents and Children.* Cambridge, MA: Barefoot Books, 2004.

Bernstein, G., Layne, A. and Egan, E. (2005). School-based interventions for anxious children. *Journal of the American Academy of Child and Adolescent Psychiatry.* 44 (11), 1118–1127.

Bersma, D. *Yoga Games for Children.* Alameda, CA: Hunter House, 2003.

Bienenfeld, F. *Helping Your Child Through Your Divorce.* Alameda, CA: Hunter House, 1995.

Carey, D., and Large, J. *Festivals, Family and Food.* Gloucestershire, England: Hawthorn Press, 1982 (available from St. George Bookstore, PO Box 225, Spring Valley, NY 10977).

Cave, C., and Maland, N. *You've Got Dragons.* Atlanta: Peachtree, 2003. (A young boy discovers that he has worries and fears that appear to him as dragons and shares what he learns about living with them)

Carouvian, R. and Sharn, O. *Child Honoring: How to Turn This World Around.* Westport, CT: Praeger, 2006.

Chansky, T. *Freeing Your Child from Obsessive-Compulsive Disorder.* New York: Crown, 2001.

Cherlin, A.J. *Marriage, Divorce and Remarriage.* Cambridge, MA: Harvard Univ. Press, 1992.

Chess, S. and Thomas, A. *Temperament: Theory and Practice,* 2nd Ed. New York: Psychology Press, 1996.

Csikszentmihalyi, M. Flow: *The Psychology of Optimal Experience.* New York: Harper and Row, 1990.

Childre, D. and Martin, H. *The HeartMath Solution.* San Francisco: Harper, 2000.

Childre, D. and Rozman, D. *Transforming Anxiety: The HeartMath Solution for Overcoming Fear and Worry and Creating Serenity.* Oakland, CA: New Harbinger, 2006.

Cohan, S., Chavira, D., and Stein, M.B. (2006). "Practitioner Review: Psychosocial interventions for children with selective mutism: a critical evaluation of the literature from 1990–2005." *Journal of Child Psychology and Psychiatry,* 47:11, 1085–1097.

Cohen, L. *The Opposite of Worry: The Playful Parenting Approach to Childhood Anxieties and Fears.* NY: Random House, 2013.

Covey, S. *The 7 Habits of Happy Kids.* NY: Simon and Schuster, 2008.

Covey, S. *The 7 Habits of Highly Effective Teens.* NY: Fireside, 1998.

Covey, S., Merrill, A. and Merrill, R. *First Things First.* New York: Fireside, 1994.

Crawford, C. *The Highly Intuitive Child.* Alameda, CA: Hunter House, 2009.

Crockenberg, S. and Leerkes, E. (2006). "Infant temperament (reactivity to novelty) and maternal behavior at 6 months interact to predict later anxious behavior." *Development and Psychopathology,* 18, 1–18.

Csikszentmihalyi, M. *Flow: The Psychology of Optimal Experience.* New York: Harper and Row, 1990.

Datillo, F., 2006. "Throwing Away the Script: Helping trainees trust their gut." *Psychotherapy Networker,* 30 (1) 27–29.

David, M. *The Slow Down Diet.* Rochester, NY: Inner Traditions, 2005.

De Shazer, S. *Clues: Investigating Solutions in Brief Therapy.* New York: Norton, 1988.

Desmond, L. *Baby Buddhas: A Guide to Teaching Meditation to Children.* Kansas City, MO: McMeel Publishing, 2004.

Diagnostic and Statistical Manual of Mental Disorders-5th Edition (DSM-5). Arlington, VA: The American Psychiatric Association, 2013.

Elkind, D. *The Hurried Child: Growing Up Too Fast and Too Soon.* Reading, MA: Addison-Wesley, 1981.

Elkind, D. *Ties That Stress: The New Family Imbalance.* Cambridge, MA: Harvard, 1994.

Epstein, M. *The Trauma of Everyday Life.* New York: Penguin, 2014.

Evans, P. *Teen Torment: Overcoming Verbal Abuse at Home and at School.* Avon, MA: Adams Media, 2003.

Felitti, J. et. al. The Adverse Childhood Experiences (ACE) Study. *Journal of Preventive Medicine.* May 1998, Volume 14, Issue 4, Pages 245–258.

Ferber, R. *Solve Your Child's Sleep Problems (Rev. Ed.).* New York: Fireside Books, 2006.

Flynn, L. *Yoga 4 Classrooms.* Dover, NH: Yoga 4 Classrooms, 2012.

Flynn, L. *Yoga for Children: 200+ Yoga Poses, Breathing Exercises, and Meditations for Healthier, Happier, More Resilient Children.* Avon, MA: Adams Media, 2013.

Foxman, P. *Dancing with Fear: Controlling Stress and Creating a Life Beyond Panic and Anxiety.* Alameda, CA: Hunter House, 2007.

Foxman, P. *The Worried Child: Recognizing Anxiety in Children and Helping Them Heal.* Alameda, CA: Hunter House, 2004.

Franke, L. G. *Growing Up Divorced: How to Help Your Children Cope with Every Stage from Infancy through Teens*. New York: Fawcett Crest, 1983.

Fromm, E. *The Gates of Repentance*. New York: Central Conference of American Rabbis, 1978.

Gardner, H. *Intelligence Reframed: Multiple Intelligences for the 21st Century*. New York: Basic Books, 2000.

Gibran, K. *The Prophet*. New York: Knopf, 1923.

Glatzer, J. *Overcoming Panic and Anxiety Disorders* (Foreword and Commentaries by Paul Foxman, Ph.D). Alameda, CA: Hunter House, 2003.

Golomb, R. and Vavrichek, S. *The Hair Pulling Habit and You: How to Solve the Trichotillomania Puzzle (Rev. Ed.)*. Washington, DC: Writer's Coop of Greater Washington, 2000.

Goodman, T. "Working with Children: Beginner's Mind." In Germer, C., Siegel, R., and Fulton, P. (Eds.) *Mindfulness and Psychotherapy*. New York: Guilford Press, 2005.

Goodyear-Brown, P. "Strategic Play Therapy Techniques for Anxious Preschoolers." In Schaefer, C., (Ed.). *Play therapy for preschool children*. Washington, D.C.: American Psychological Association, 2010.

Greenberger, D. and Padesky, C. *Mind Over Mood: A Cognitive Therapy Treatment Manual for Clients*. New York: Guilford, 1995.

Greenland, S. *The Mindful Child: How to Help Your Child Manage Stress and Become Happier, Kinder and More Compassionate*. New York: Free Press, 2010.

Greenwald, R. *Eye Movement Desensitization and Reprocessing (EMDR) in Child and Adolescent Psychotherapy*. Northvale, NJ: Aronson, 1999.

Greenwald, R. (1998). "Eye movement desensitization and reprocessing (EMDR): New hope for children suffering from trauma and loss." *Clinical Child Psychology and Psychiatry*, 3, 279–287.

Gruenwald, J. *PDR for Herbal Medicine*, 3rd Ed., Montvale, NY: Tomlinson PDR, 2004.

Hammond, D. (2005). "Neurofeedback with anxiety and affective disorders." *Child and Adolescent Psychiatric Clinics of North America*, 14 (1): 105–123.

Hanh, T. N., Nghiem, C., and Vriezen, W. *Planting Seeds: Practicing Mindfulness with Children*. Berkeley, CA: Parallax Press, 2011.

Henkes, K. *Wemberly Worried*. New York: Greenwillow, 2000.

Hill, K. and Wigfield, A. (1984) Test Anxiety: A Major Educational Problem and What Can Be Done about It. *The Elementary School Journal*, Vol. 85, No. 1, Special Issue: Motivation. Sep., pp. 105–126.

Hilliard, E. *Living Fully with Shyness and Social Anxiety: A Comprehensive Guide to Gaining Social Confidence*. New York: Marlowe, 2005.

Holmes, T, and Rahe, R. (1967). "The Social Readjustment Rating Scale". *J Psychosom Res* 11 (2): 213–8.

House, R. "Foreword" in Evans, R. *Helping Children to Overcome Fear*. Gloucester, England: Hawthorn Press, 2000.

Huebner, D. *What to Do When You Worry Too Much: A Kids Guide to Overcoming Anxiety*. Washington, DC: Magination, 2006.

Huebner, D. *What to Do When Your Brain Gets Stuck: A Kids Guide to Overcoming OCD*. Washington, DC: Magination, 2007.

Jenkinson, S. *The Genius of Play: Celebrating the Spirit of Childhood*. Gloucester, England: Hawthorn Press, 2001.

Kelly, J. (2007) Children's Living Arrangements Following Separation and Divorce: Insights from Empirical and Clinical Research. *Family Process*, 46: 35–52.

Kelly, J. (2005). Developing Beneficial Parenting Plan Models for Children Following Separation and Divorce. *J. of the American Academy of Matrimonial Lawyers*, 19: 237–254.

Kendall, P. *Cognitive-Behavioral Therapy for Anxious Children: Therapist Manual*. Ardmore, PA: Workbook Publishing, 1990.

Kendall, P. *Coping Cat Workbook*. Ardmore, PA: Workbook Publishing, 1992.

Kramer, S. *Guided Meditation for Children*. Santa Barbara, CA: Creations in Consciousness, 2003.

Kranowitz, C. *The Out-of-Sync Child: Revised Edition*. New York: Perigree, 2005.

Kristol, J. *The Temperament Perspective: Working With Children's Behavioral Styles*. Baltimore. Brookes Pub., 2004.

Keuthen, N., Stein, D., and Christenson, G. *Help for Hair Pullers: Understanding and Coping with Trichotillomania*. Oakland, CA: New Harbinger, 2001.

Lahey, J. *The Gift of Failure: How the Best Parents Learn to Let Go So Their Children Can Succeed*. New York: HarperCollins, 2015.

Levin, D. and Kilbourne, J. *So Sexy, So Soon: The New Sexualized Childhood and What Parents Can do to Protect Their Kids*. New York: Ballantine, 2008.

Lambert, M. Implications of outcome research for psychotherapy integration. In Norcross, J. and Goldfried, M. (Eds.), *Handbook of psychotherapy integration*, (pp. 94–129). New York: Basic Books, 1992.

Lane, F. *Cybertraps for the Young*. Chicago: NTI Upstream, 2011.

Lidell, L. *The Sivananda Companion to Yoga*. New York: Simon and Schuster, 1983.

Linn, S. *The Case for Make Believe: Saving Play in a Commercialized World*. New York: New Press, 2008.

Louv, R. *Last Child In the Woods: Saving Our Children from Nature-Deficit Disorder*. Chapel Hill: Algonquin, 2008.

March, J., and Mulle, K. *OCD in Children and Adolescents: A Cognitive-Behavioral Therapy Manual*. New York: Guilford, 1998.

McGoldrick, M., Gerson, R. and Shellenberger, S. *Genograms: Assessment and Intervention,* 2nd Ed. New York: Norton, 1999.

McGraw, J. *Life Strategies for Teens.* NY: Fireside, 2000.

McHolm, A, Cunningham, C., and Vanier, M. *Helping Your Child with Selective Mutism: Steps to Overcome a Fear of Speaking.* Oakland, CA: New Harbinger, 2005.

Moser, A. *Don't Feed the Monster on Tuesdays! The Children's Self-Esteem Book.* Kansas City: Landmark, 1991.

Pearce, J. *Magical Child: Rediscovering Nature's Plan for Our Children.* New York: Dutton, 1977.

Pearce, J. *The Biology of Transcendence.* Rochester, VT: Park Street Press, 2002.

Penzel, F. *The Hair-Pulling Problem: A Complete Guide to Trichotillomania.* New York: Oxford University Press, 2003.

Phalen, T. *1-2-3 Magic: Effective Discipline for Children 2-12.* Glen Ellyn, IL: ParentMagic, 2004.

Phillips, D. *How to Give Your Child a Great Self-Image.* New York: Plume, 1991.

Piaget, J. *The Origins of Intelligence in Children.* New York: Norton, 1952.

Postman, N. *The Disappearance of Childhood.* New York: Vintage: 1994.

Przybylski, A. Electronic Gaming and Psychosocial Adjustment. *Pediatrics*, July, 2014.

Purperhart, H. *The Yoga Adventure for Children: Playing, Dancing, Moving, Breathing, Relaxing.* Alameda, CA: Hunter House, 2006.

Quart, A. *Branded: The Buying and Selling of Teenagers.* Cambridge, MA: Perseus, 2003.

Rapaport, J. *The Boy Who Couldn't Stop Washing.* New York: Signet, 1991.

Rapee, R., Wignall, A, Spence, S., and Cobham, V. *Helping Your Anxious Child: A Step-by-Step Guide for Parents.* Oakland, CA: New Harbinger, 2008.

Ratey, J. and Hagerman, E. *Spark: The Revolutionary New Science of Exercise and the Brain.* New York: Little, Brown, 2008.

Reynolds, C., and Richmond, B. *Revised Children's Manifest Anxiety Scale.* Los Angeles, CA: Western Psychological Services, 1985.

Rosenfeld, A. and Wise, N. *The Over-Scheduled Child: Avoiding the Hyper-Parenting Trap.* New York: St. Martin's Press, 2000.

Rueben, S. *But How Will You Raise Your Children? A Guide to Interfaith Marriage.* New York: Pocket Books, 1987.

SAMHSA (Substance Abuse and Mental Health Services Administration). *Results from the 2011 National Survey on Drug Use and Health: Summary of National Findings,* NSDUH Series H-44, HHS Publication No. (SMA) 12-4713. Rockville, MD: Substance Abuse and Mental Health Services Administration, 2012.

Satir, V. *Conjoint Family Therapy.* Palo Alto, CA: Science and Behavior Books, 1983a.

Satir, V, and Baldwin, M. *Satir Step By Step: A Guide to Creating Change in Families.* Palo Alto, CA: Science and Behavior Books, 1983b.

Schwartz, J. *Brainlock: Free Yourself from Obsessive-Compulsive Behavior.* New York: Regan Books, 1996.

Selekman, M. *Solution-Focused Therapy with Children: Harnessing Family Strengths for Systemic Change.* New York: Guilford, 1997.

Siegel, D. and Bryson, T. *The Whole Brain Child: 12 Revolutionary Strategies for Nurturing Your Child's Developing Mind, Survive Everyday Struggles, and Help Your Family Thrive.* New York: Delacorte, 2011.

Silverman, W. and Ollendick, T. (2005). Evidence-based assessment of anxiety and its disorders in children and adolescents. *Journal of Clinical Child and Adolescen Psychoogy*. Sept, (3):380-411.

Stewart, M. *Yoga for Children.* New York: Fireside, 1992.

Syed, M. *Bounce: Mozart, Federer, Picasso, Beckham and the Science of Success.* New York: HarperCollins, 2010.

Terr, L. *Too Scared to Cry: How Trauma Affects Children and Ultimately Us All.* New York: Basic Books, 1992.

Tinker, R. and Wilson, S. *Through the Eyes of a Child: EMDR with Children.* New York: Norton, 1999.

Tough, P. *How Children Succeed: Grit, Curiosity, and the Hidden Power of Character.* New York: Houghton Mifflin Harcourt, 2012.

Turner, B., Beidel, D., Hughes, S., and Turner, M. (1993). Test anxiety in African American school children. *School Psychology Quarterly*, 8, 140–152.

Valenstein, E. *Blaming the Brain: The Truth about Drugs and Mental Health.* New York: Free Press, 1998.

Viorst, J. *Necessary Losses: The Loves, Illusions, Dependencies and Impossible Expectations That All of Us Have to Give Up in Order to Grow.* New York: Fireside, 1986.

Wagner, A. *Treatment of OCD in Children and Adolescents: A Cognitive-Behavioral Therapy Manual.* Rochester, NY: Lighthouse Press, 2003.

Wagner, A. *What to Do When Your Child Has Obsessive-Compulsive Disorder: Strategies and Solutions.* Lighthouse Point, FL: Lighthouse, Press, 2002.

Wallerstein, J., and Blakeslee, S. *What About the Kids? Raising Your Children Before, During, and After Divorce.* New York: Hyperion, 2003.

Wampold, B. *The Great Psychotherapy Debate: Models, Methods and Findings.* Mahwah, NJ: Erlbaum, 2008.

Weekes, C. (1978). Simple, Effective Treatment of Agoraphobia. *American Journal of Psychotherapy* 23(3), 357–69.

Wilens, T. *Straight Talk About Psychiatric Medications for Children.* New York: Guildford, 2002.

Zimbardo, P. and Shirly, R. *The Shy Child: Overcoming and Preventing Shyness from Infancy to Adulthood.* New York: Addison-Wesley, 1997.